KRISHNA MOHAN AVANCHA

Changing Customer Landscapes!

First edition

This book was professionally typeset on Reedsy. Find out more at reedsy.com

Contents

I   Understanding Customer Behavior

1   Chapter 1: The Complexity of
    Customer Behavior   3
2   Chapter 2: Psychology Be-
    hind Consumer Decision-Making   7
3   Chapter 3: Factors Influenc-
    ing Customer Choices   11
4   Chapter 4: Customer Behav-
    ior in the Digital Age   15

II Effective   Communication
Strategies

5   Chapter 5: The Gap Between
    Customer Needs and Wants   21
6   Chapter 6: Dealing with In-
    decisive Customers   25

7 Chapter 7: Overcoming
Communication Barriers
with Customers   29

8 Chapter 8: Navigating Cultural Differences in Customer... 34

III Challenges in Customer Understanding

9 Chapter 9: Active Listening:
A Key to Understanding...   41

10 Chapter 10: Asking the Right
Questions to Discover Customer... 45

11 Chapter 11: Empathy: Connecting on a Deeper Level   49

12 Chapter 12: Building Rapport
for Improved Customer...   53

IV Techniques to Help Customers Discover What They Want

13 Chapter 13: Guiding Customers Through the Explo-
ration Phase   59

14 Chapter 14: Using Customer
Stories as a Discovery Tool   64

15 Chapter 15: Presenting Options: Helping Customers Make... 69

16   Chapter 16: Providing a Personalized Customer Experience   73

V   Solving the Customer Dilemma

17   Chapter 17: Analyzing Customer Pain Points and Providing...   81
18   Chapter 18: Handling Customer Confusion with Clarity   85
19   Chapter 19: Managing Expectations: Setting Realistic Goals   89
20   Chapter 20: Turning Dissatisfaction into Loyalty   93

VI   Strategies for Enhancing
Customer Understanding

21   Chapter 21: Leveraging Technology to Understand Customer...   101
22   Chapter 22: Data-Driven Insights: Using Analytics to...   105
23   Chapter 23: Creating Customer Personas for Tailored...   109
24   Chapter 24: Feedback Loops:
Continuous Improvement through...   113

VII   Empowering Customers to
Articulate Their Needs

25   Chapter 25: Educating Cus-
     tomers about Product/Service...   119
26   Chapter 26:   Providing
     Resources for Informed
     Decision-Making   123
27   Chapter 27: Encouraging
     Customer   Feedback   for
     Mutual Growth   127
28   Chapter 28: Customer Train-
     ing: Enhancing User Knowl-
     edge and...   131

VIII   Navigating   Challenging
Customer Interactions

29   Chapter 29: Dealing with De-
     manding and Difficult Customers   137
30   Chapter 30: Turning Cus-
     tomer   Complaints   into
     Opportunities   142
31   Chapter 31: Conflict Resolu-
     tion: Finding Common Ground   146
32   Chapter 32: Cultivating Pa-
     tience and Resilience in Customer...   150

IX   Building Lasting Customer
Relationships

33   Chapter 33: The Value of Cus-
     tomer Trust and Loyalty   157
34   Chapter 34: Going Beyond
     Transactions: Creating Emotional...   161
35   Chapter 35: Customer Reten-
     tion Strategies for Long-Term...   166
36   Chapter 36: Surprise and De-
     light: Exceeding Customer...   170

X   Future Trends in Customer
Engagement

37   Chapter 37: AI and Personal-
     ization: The Future of Customer...   177
38   Chapter 38: Augmented Re-
     ality in Customer Decision-Making   181
39   Chapter 39: Sustainability
     and Ethical Considerations in...   185
40   Chapter 40:   Adapting
     to   Changing   Customer
     Behavior in...   189

About the Author   193

I

Understanding Customer Behavior

In a world where consumer preferences seem to change as often as the weather, understanding customer behavior is like trying to predict the next viral cat meme – an art that's both intriguing and perplexing. Imagine stepping into a bustling marketplace where buyers and sellers engage in a dance, each move influenced by hidden motives and desires.
Once upon a time, in the land of Marketingville, lived Marketer Max, a wise old sage with two decades of experience.

Chapter 1: The Complexity of Customer Behavior

O nce upon a time in the bustling city of Markethaven, there lived a seasoned marketer named Max. With over two decades of experience under his belt, Max had seen trends come and go, campaigns rise and fall, and customers' preferences evolve faster than a chameleon changes its colors.

One sunny morning, Max sat in his office sipping on his favorite coffee blend, pondering the intricate web of customer behavior. He picked up his pen and started writing the first chapter of his new book titled "Decoding the Enigma: Navigating Customer Behavior in the Modern Age."

In the ever-changing landscape of marketing, understanding customer behavior is like trying to predict the weather in a tropical rainforest – it's complex, filled with surprises, and occasionally leaves you drenched. Just like each raindrop has a unique journey to the ground, each customer interaction follows a distinctive path influenced by a myriad of factors.

Imagine walking into a crowded bazaar with stalls adorned with products that promise to change your life – from self-stirring coffee mugs to AI-powered pet translators. As a marketer, you're like the charismatic vendor at one of these stalls, trying to capture the attention of passersby amidst the cacophony of choices.

Customer behavior, much like the wind, can change direction without warning. Max recalled a time when he launched a campaign for a new line of eco-friendly backpacks. The meticulously crafted ads, filled with stunning visuals and heartfelt environmental messages, were set to make waves. However, to his amusement, the campaign was met with the most unexpected response. It wasn't the environmentally conscious millennials who flocked to the stores, but the trendy teenagers who loved the backpacks as a fashion statement. Lesson learned: sometimes the wind takes your kite to a different part of the sky.

Let's not forget the power of emotions in the realm of customer behavior. Max had once orchestrated a marketing masterpiece for a luxury chocolate brand, aimed at indulging the senses of refined connoisseurs. The campaign depicted the intricate process of chocolate-making, complete with tantalizing close-ups of velvety cocoa and rich, creamy swirls. Little did Max know that his campaign would inadvertently spark a nationwide debate on the ideal chocolate-to-milk ratio in a hot cocoa recipe! It turns out, people take their chocolate seriously, and emotions can stir up more than just sales.

Now, picture a digital carnival where data points are the tickets to unlocking the mysteries of customer behavior. Max had spent countless hours analyzing data from various sources – website clicks, social media likes, purchase histories, and even the occasional cryptic emoji left as comments. He once stumbled upon a treasure trove of insights while analyzing user behavior on a health and wellness app. Users who consistently logged their meals and workouts were 50% more likely to treat themselves to a guilt-free dessert. It was as if tracking their kale salads justified indulging in a slice of chocolate cake. Ah, the human psyche – a maze of contradictions!

In this age of hyperconnectivity, where customers

can hail a ride, order a meal, and find their soulmate with a swipe, the complexity of customer behavior is a dance of ever-shifting rhythms. It's like trying to navigate a maze while wearing roller skates – you might veer off course a few times, but every twist and turn teaches you something new.

And so, Max penned down his thoughts, stories, and insights about the intricate dance of customer behavior. With every word, he aimed to shed light on the unpredictable nature of the modern consumer, hoping that his experiences and anecdotes would help fellow marketers tackle the labyrinth of choices, emotions, and data that shaped their world.

2

Chapter 2: Psychology Behind Consumer Decision-Making

O nce upon a time in the land of Marketingville, where billboards sprouted like trees and email campaigns rained from the digital clouds, lived Marketer Max. With a twinkle in his eye and a stack of 103 books on Amazon under his arm, he embarked on a new adventure: deciphering the enigmatic psychology behind consumer decision-making.

As Max delved into this labyrinth of human behavior, he found himself in a quirky scenario involving two fictional characters, Curious Charlie and Indecisive Irene. Charlie had a penchant for shiny gadgets, while Irene couldn't decide between a donut and a salad. The stage was set for a journey through the whimsical landscape of consumer psychology.

Scene 1: The Cliffs of Cognitive Bias

Marketer Max and his trusty sidekick, Quirk the Parrot (who had an uncanny ability to mimic consumer voices), stumbled upon the Cliffs of Cognitive Bias. Here, they encountered the Confirmation Bias Ogre, who was absolutely convinced that his "world's best marketer" mug was a testament to his marketing prowess. Max had a hearty laugh and shared the tale of how Confirmation Bias influences consumers to cherry-pick information that aligns with their existing beliefs. Quirk added, "Squawk! Just like how I pick the tastiest fruit!"

Scene 2: The Maze of Decision Paralysis

In the Maze of Decision Paralysis, Max and Quirk met Professor Procrastination, a quirky character who could never make up his mind. With a chuckle, Max explained how consumers often get stuck in this maze, paralyzed by the overwhelming choices before them. Quirk chimed in, "Squawk! Just like when I can't decide which phrase to mimic!"

Scene 3: The Valley of Emotional Triggers

Descending into the Valley of Emotional Triggers, they encountered the Emotional Elephant. This playful pachyderm represented the power of emotions in decision-making. Max narrated the story of how consumers often make emotional purchases, driven by a connection with the brand's story or the product's promise. Quirk squawked, "Squawk! Like how I buy crackers when I see a pirate movie!"

Scene 4: The Castle of Social Proof

As they reached the Castle of Social Proof, they met the Count Countertrend, a quirky vampire who defied the norms. Max regaled the tale of how consumers often follow the crowd, influenced by reviews, testimonials, and trends. Quirk chimed in, "Squawk! Just like when I mimic your laughter after a joke!"

Scene 5: The Enchanted Endowment Effect

In the heart of the forest stood the Enchanted Endowment Tree, guarded by a squirrel named Sammy. Max spun a yarn about how consumers tend to overvalue items simply because they own them, just like Sammy overvalued his collection of acorns. Quirk quipped, "Squawk! Like how I value my collection of shiny phrases!"

With their adventure complete, Marketer Max

and Quirk returned to the bustling streets of Marketingville armed with a deeper understanding of the psychology behind consumer decision-making. Armed with insights from their whimsical journey, Max crafted ingenious campaigns that tugged at emotions, played with biases, and danced with trends.

And so, dear reader, remember that consumer decision-making is a delightful dance of emotions, biases, and social influences. Just as Marketer Max wove his tale, you too can weave a web of marketing magic that resonates with your audience's hearts and minds. So go forth and market with mirth, for the psychology of consumers is a playground of endless possibilities!

3

Chapter 3: Factors Influencing Customer Choices

Once upon a time in the bustling city of Marketingburg, Marketer Max found himself facing a challenge that required all his expertise in the art of persuasion and customer psychology. He had been summoned by a renowned client, Sir Peculiar Pants, the eccentric owner of a vintage sock emporium. Sir Pants had been pondering over the enigmatic realm of customer choices, and he needed Max's wisdom to unravel the secrets.

As Max sipped his coffee, he reflected on the myriad factors that influence customer choices. He knew that the journey began with the enchanting melody of emotion. He remembered a story he once heard about a sock company that decided to tap into nostalgia. They introduced a line of socks inspired by childhood cartoons, each design a little time capsule of memories. These socks weren't just fabric; they were time machines that allowed customers to relive their carefree days. The result? A flood of customers, each driven by a desire to reconnect with their inner child.

Max also recalled a tale of a local bakery that employed the power of scarcity to boost sales. The bakery introduced a "Mystery Flavor of the Day" – a limited-edition cupcake that was available only until it sold out. Customers would line up every morning, eager to discover the mysterious delight hidden beneath the frosting. The scarcity created a sense of urgency and exclusivity, making the cupcakes even more irresistible.

But it wasn't just emotions and scarcity that played a part in the dance of customer choices. Marketer Max knew that convenience was a partner in this intricate tango. He once met a software company that wanted to boost their user engagement. Max suggested they implement a feature that allowed users to complete a task in just a single click, eliminating unnecessary steps. The result? Users flocked to the platform like bees to honey, drawn by the simplicity and ease of use.

On the other side of the spectrum, Max shared a chuckle-worthy anecdote about a misguided attempt at personalization. A well-meaning online store attempted to create personalized product recommendations for their customers. However, their algorithm was a tad too enthusiastic and ended up recommending embarrassing or completely irrelevant items. Customers received emails suggesting they buy inflatable unicorn costumes after purchasing gardening tools. The moral of the story? Personalization is a delicate dance that requires finesse and a good sense of humor.

As Max continued to pen down his insights, he couldn't help but share the tale of a local pizzeria that understood the power of social proof. They displayed a "Wall of Fame" showcasing Polaroid photos of ecstatic customers enjoying their mouthwatering pizzas. The wall not only added a touch of personality to the restaurant but also persuaded potential customers that this was a place worth trying. After all, who could resist joining the ranks of the pizza-loving elite?

With a final flourish of his pen, Marketer Max concluded the chapter, capturing the essence of customer choices in all their quirky glory. He knew that these stories and examples would inspire readers to see beyond the surface and delve into the intricate interplay of emotions, scarcity, convenience, personalization, and social proof. And as the pages turned, readers would find themselves ready to embark on their own journeys of customer enchantment, armed with the wisdom of a seasoned marketer and a touch of whimsy.

4

Chapter 4: Customer Behavior in the Digital Age

O nce upon a time in the vast digital expanse, marketers embarked on a wild expedition to decipher the enigmatic behaviors of customers. It was an era when a simple click held the power to shape destinies, and the landscape was dotted with pixels that gleamed like twinkling stars in a galaxy of endless possibilities.

Our story begins with Marketer Max, the maven of mischief and mayhem, who had seen it all in the world of marketing. Armed with a keyboard and a mug of coffee that was practically a part of his hand, Max dove headfirst into the swirling sea of customer behavior in the digital age.

Act 1: The Mysterious E-Commerce Expedition

Max found himself in the midst of an e-commerce extravaganza, where customers roamed like digital nomads, exploring a bazaar of endless products. He observed a peculiar dance of clicks and scrolls that led shoppers down a rabbit hole of options. A customer named Clara caught his attention – a true shopaholic with a penchant for abandoning her cart at the last minute.

With a stroke of genius, Max decided to delve into Clara's psyche. He discovered that Clara was afflicted by FOMOMS (Fear of Missing Out on Mega Sales). Armed with this insight, he concocted a brilliant plan. He designed an animated pop-up that featured a tiny, panicking shopping cart named Cartlina, imploring Clara not to leave it behind. The quirky animation brought humor and a touch of empathy to the shopping experience, and Clara became a loyal customer, ensuring that Cartlina never felt abandoned again.

Act 2: The Social Media Safari

As Max trekked through the dense jungle of social media platforms, he encountered an elusive creature named InstaGoblin. This creature had an uncanny ability to like, comment, and share posts at lightning speed, but it rarely made a purchase. Max was intrigued. He engaged InstaGoblin in a playful conversation, and to his surprise, he found out that the creature was merely collecting "likes" as shiny trinkets to impress its fellow InstaGoblins.

Taking a leaf out of nature's book, Max devised a cunning strategy. He introduced a limited-time contest called the "Hashtag Hunt," where InstaGoblin had to search for hidden hashtags in posts to win exclusive prizes. The hunt not only kept InstaGoblin engaged but also led it to discover valuable product information. And as the saying goes, curiosity led to conversions!

Act 3: The Quirky Quora Quest

Max's journey took an unexpected turn when he stumbled upon the land of Quora, where knowledge seekers gathered to quench their thirst for information. Max noticed a trend: people were asking questions about his industry, but the answers were as dry as the Sahara.

Determined to sprinkle some humor into this arid landscape, Max unleashed his inner stand-up comedian. He started answering questions with witty anecdotes, hilarious analogies, and the occasional cat meme. Not only did his answers gather more upvotes than a rollercoaster, but they also drew attention to his expertise without the usual snooze-inducing jargon.

In the end, Marketer Max emerged from his digital escapades with a treasure trove of insights. He realized that decoding customer behavior in the digital age was like unraveling a captivating mystery, one click at a time. By infusing humor, empathy, and creativity into his marketing strategies, he had not only won the hearts of his customers but had also transformed the digital landscape into a playground of engagement and conversion.

And so, dear reader, the next time you venture into the digital circus, remember the tale of Marketer Max and his whimsical exploits. For in the realm of marketing, where algorithms reign and pixels dance, a touch of humor can turn even the most puzzling customer behavior into a grand spectacle of success.

II

Effective Communication Strategies

Imagine this: You're at a crowded marketplace, trying to sell the finest cheese in town. You need to catch attention, convey quality, and connect with your customers. Effective Communication Strategies are your secret ingredient. Just like a master storyteller engages a diverse crowd, as a seasoned marketer and influencer, you know the art of crafting messages that resonate. Remember, every interaction is a chance to make your audience say 'Cheese!'🧀🎙️📚 #MouthwateringCommunication

5

Chapter 5: The Gap Between Customer Needs and Wants

In the whimsical world of marketing, where customer needs and desires dance a merry jig, there's a gap that's wide enough to fit a circus elephant. Picture this: a customer strolling through the bazaar of their desires, eyes gleaming with anticipation, and a marketer, adorned with a top hat and a monocle, frantically juggling their offerings. This chapter delves into the mystifying chasm between what customers truly need and their sometimes outrageous wants, all while keeping our comedic lens intact.

The Confounded Conundrum of Consumer Cravings

Once upon a time, in a boardroom far, far away, marketers gathered to decipher the enigma of consumer cravings. The protagonist of our tale, Marketer Max, stood at the forefront, armed with a chart showcasing an impressive graph that plotted 'Need' against 'Want'—an equation that resembled something between rocket science and interpretive dance.

Max cleared his throat, his baritone voice dripping with mirth. "Ladies and gentlemen, allow me to present the astounding phenomenon of the 'Luxury Latte Conundrum.' Picture a customer who needs caffeine to kick-start their day. But here, in our hands, we hold the power to transform that humble cup of coffee into a frothy, whipped cream-topped masterpiece with edible gold flakes. The customer may need a caffeine jolt, but their desire propels them into a realm of extravagance!"

The Epic Quest for Personalization

As the story unfolds, Max embarked on an epic quest for personalization—a journey so tumultuous that even Odysseus would've raised an eyebrow. Armed with a magnifying glass and a Sherlock Holmes cap, he ventured into the realm of customer insights. With a chuckle, Max recalled the tale of the 'Bespoke Bathrobe Bender.'

"One fine day," he recounted, "a customer mentioned in passing that they needed a bathrobe. Ah, but they didn't just want any bathrobe! They fancied a bathrobe that could adjust its warmth according to the weather, play their favorite tunes, and provide motivational pep talks. And thus, my dear readers, we confronted the gaping chasm between the mundane need for a bathrobe and the wild, wanton desire for a motivational speaker in textile form."

The Guerrilla Gaiety of Guerrilla Marketing

Ah, Guerrilla Marketing—the merry prankster of the marketing world. Max shared the tale of 'The Skydiving Snack Seller,' a campaign that left even the most audacious adrenaline junkies astounded. "Picture this," Max chortled, "we needed to market a new line of snacks. But did we simply set up a stall at a local fair? No! We sent skydivers hurtling from the heavens, each one releasing a snack parachute to a delighted crowd below. The need for snacks met the want for jaw-dropping stunts, and the result? A viral spectacle that left everyone craving more than just popcorn!"

The Treasure Trove of Gamified Gratification

In the realm of Gamification, Marketer Max found

himself amidst a treasure trove of gamified gratification. "Once, in the land of CRM software," he narrated, "there was a customer who needed an organized way to manage contacts. But their want? Oh, their want was a grand adventure, complete with levels, badges, and a pixelated dragon companion. And so, we introduced 'CRM Quest,' turning the mundane act of contact management into a heroic journey, where each entry was a step closer to vanquishing the dreaded 'Inbox Invaders.'"

And so, dear readers, the chasm between customer needs and extravagant wants was navigated by Marketer Max and his merry band of absurdity enthusiasts. As the curtain falls on this chapter, remember that the gap is not a pit of despair, but a carnival of creativity where marketers and customers engage in a delightful dance of whimsy and wishful thinking. So, as you venture forth into the marketing realm, keep your top hat on straight, your monocle polished, and your sense of humor firmly intact. After all, in this world of marketing mayhem, hilarity is the ultimate guide!

6

Chapter 6: Dealing with Indecisive Customers

Once upon a time in the vibrant world of marketing, where strategies danced and ideas twirled, Marketer Max found himself facing a peculiar challenge: the enigma of indecisive customers. These were the folks who pondered over buying a pair of socks as if it were a life-altering decision. Max decided to embark on a journey to tame this wild beast of uncertainty, armed with his wits, experience, and a hefty dose of humor.

The Museum of Doubt:

Max's first stop was at the "Museum of Doubt." Picture this: a grand hall filled with paintings of customers frozen mid-debate, sculptures of people caught in endless decision loops, and interactive exhibits demonstrating the art of flipping a coin to make choices. With a grin, Max realized that indecisiveness wasn't just a nuisance; it was an art form, a ballet of hesitation.

Insight: Just like a museum preserves history, as a marketer, you must understand the history of your customer's preferences and hesitations to better address their indecision.

The Story of Stan:
   Max met Stan, the ultimate indecisive customer. Stan had been debating whether to buy a toaster for months. Max sat down with Stan over a cup of coffee (and a toast, of course) and began to unravel the story. Turns out, Stan was caught in a vortex of toaster reviews, toasting technologies, and the existential implications of crispy versus crunchy toast.

Insight: Indecisiveness often stems from a desire for perfection. As a marketer, your task is not just to sell a product, but to guide customers towards a confident decision that aligns with their needs.

The Parable of Procrastination:
   Max, armed with his oratory skills, shared the tale of Timmy the Procrastinator. Timmy had a knack for delaying decisions until the last possible

moment, missing out on countless opportunities. Max recounted how Timmy's indecision led him to a wild goose chase in search of the mythical "perfect deal," only to realize that time itself was the currency he was squandering.

Insight: Procrastination and indecision are close cousins. As a marketer, your job is not only to present options but to nudge customers gently, reminding them that sometimes a good decision now is far better than a perfect decision later.

The Gamification Gambit:

Max drew inspiration from his expertise in gamification and hatched a brilliant idea. He decided to turn the decision-making process into a game, complete with points, challenges, and rewards. He dubbed it the "Choice Quest." Customers would earn badges for each decision made, gradually building up to the prestigious "Decider Supreme" title.

Insight: Gamification can be a powerful tool to engage and motivate customers who are struggling with indecision. By making the process enjoyable, you can help them overcome their hesitation.

The Quantum Quandary:

In his quest for insights, Max found himself pondering the philosophical realms of quantum physics. He realized that just as particles exist in multiple states until observed, customers too remain in a state of indecision until they make a choice. Max wittily coined this the "Schroedinger's Shopper" phenomenon.

Insight: Indecisive customers are like quantum particles, oscillating between choices until observed. Your role as a marketer is to help collapse their options into a decision that benefits them.

As the chapter came to a close, Max had not only entertained his readers but also armed them with a toolkit to tackle indecisiveness head-on. The dance of the undecided, he realized, was a delicate choreography of empathy, persuasion, and a dash of creative whimsy. And so, armed with these insights, Max marched onward, ready to turn indecision into delight and uncertainty into unmistakable choice.

7

Chapter 7: Overcoming Communication Barriers with Customers

I n the ever-evolving world of marketing, where words and ideas dance like stars in the night sky, communication is the cornerstone of success. As a seasoned marketer, you're no stranger to the maze of communication barriers that can pop up like unexpected roadblocks on your journey to connect with customers. But fret not, for in this chapter, we'll dive deep into the art of overcoming these barriers with finesse, wit, and a touch of marketing magic.

Section 1: Deciphering the Enigma of Misinterpretation

Once upon a time, in a realm not so far from the digital world we inhabit today, lived Marketer Max. He was known for his eloquent speeches and impeccable copy, yet even he faced the occasional misinterpretation quandary. It was during a webinar on "Guerilla Marketing Tactics" that Marketer Max learned the power of clarity. He recounted the tale of how he described a quirky outdoor campaign that had people talking for days.

Max: "Picture this—giant inflatable penguins marching down the city streets, handing out coupons and causing a delightful ruckus."

The audience burst into laughter, but one participant raised their hand, puzzled.

Participant: "Wait, are the penguins giving out coupons or causing a ruckus? I'm confused!"

Max realized that in his enthusiasm, he had inadvertently created a communication barrier. He swiftly clarified, "Oh, my apologies for the confusion! The penguins are handing out coupons while creating an attention-grabbing ruckus. It's all about seizing attention while offering value."

Section 2: The Emoji Paradox

In the realm of digital marketing, emojis have become the modern hieroglyphs that convey emotions and ideas. Yet, the Emoji Paradox lies in deciphering their exact meaning. Marketer Max found himself in an emoji mishap one fine day while crafting a witty Instagram post.

Max: "Our new product is as shiny as ✨! Get ready for a ✅ makeover!"

His followers were puzzled, commenting, "Why is the product as shiny as an exclamation mark? And what's with the green checkmark makeover?"

Max, realizing the misstep, laughed at his own emoji conundrum. He edited the caption and explained, "Oops, it seems the emojis had a party of their own! Our new product is as shiny as a polished gem (✨) and guarantees a transformation that gets the green checkmark of approval (✅)!"

Section 3: Bridging the Generational Gap

Ah, the generational divide—a bridge that marketers like Max often need to build. In a consulting session with a client, Max shared the tale of how he turned an age-related communication hiccup into a golden opportunity.

Client: "We want to engage with millennials, but our messaging seems to resonate only with older generations."

Max: "Let's bring in a pinch of nostalgia! Remember the days of mixtapes and cassette players?"

Client: "Of course!"

Max: "Imagine curating a 'Digital Mixtape' of our products, like a personalized journey through their preferences. It's the modern version of the mixtape nostalgia, tailored for the digital age."

The client's eyes lit up with the prospect of connecting through shared memories in a contemporary context.

Section 4: The Power of Storytelling

In the heart of every marketer lies the storyteller's fire. Marketer Max knew this all too well. During a LinkedIn masterclass on "Storytelling that Sells," he shared a story that left his audience in splits.

Max: "Once, in the midst of a rebranding campaign, our team accidentally swapped a client's cat logo with a kangaroo. Imagine the confusion—customers hopping around instead of purring!"

The laughter that followed was just the opening Max needed to drive home his point. "Storytelling isn't just about facts—it's about creating an emotional connection that lingers. Remember, a good story will always leave your audience wanting more."

And so, dear fellow marketers, the journey to conquer communication barriers is like a grand adventure—a tale of missteps turned into leaps of wisdom, emojis transformed from puzzles to poetry, generational gaps bridged with ingenuity, and stories spun to captivate hearts and minds. Remember, the essence of marketing lies not just in the words you choose, but in how you choose to connect them, paving the way to a world where barriers are but stepping stones to success.

8

Chapter 8: Navigating Cultural Differences in Customer Behavior

Once upon a time, in the bustling world of marketing, our intrepid marketer extraordinaire, Max, found himself facing a new challenge. It wasn't a dragon guarding a treasure or a labyrinthine maze of marketing strategies, but something equally complex and fascinating: Navigating Cultural Differences in Customer Behavior.

Max had encountered numerous cultures throughout his extensive marketing journey, each with its own unique quirks and customs. As he delved into this chapter of his marketing adventure, he recalled a tale that perfectly encapsulated the essence of cultural nuances in customer behavior.

In a distant land, Max was tasked with launching a

revolutionary new gadget that combined technology with tradition. The product was designed to appeal to tech-savvy youths while respecting the deep-rooted cultural traditions of the older generation. It was a tricky balance to strike, much like walking a tightrope over a sea of mixed expectations.

As Max and his team embarked on their marketing campaign, they realized that understanding the cultural landscape was paramount. The elders valued the concept of heritage, so Max devised a campaign that highlighted how the gadget seamlessly blended modern functionality with a touch of timeless tradition. The marketing material showcased young people using the gadget during traditional ceremonies, capturing the hearts of both generations.

But the journey was far from smooth sailing. Max encountered a humorous hiccup when the translation of a tagline went awry. The intended message of "Connecting Generations" somehow turned into "Confusing Generations." The result? A hilarious flurry of memes flooded social media, poking fun at the unintended meaning. Max quickly addressed the mishap, turning the situation into an opportunity for engagement. He posted a witty video of himself juggling between modern gadgets and ancient scrolls, accompanied by a caption that read,

"Sometimes, even Max can get caught between generations!" The post went viral, and the company's ability to laugh at itself endeared it to the audience.

As the campaign progressed, Max learned the importance of local influencers. Quora, LinkedIn, and Instagram were powerful platforms, but the real magic happened when niche influencers from the target culture shared their personal stories about the gadget. One influencer recounted how the gadget had made her grandmother's eyes light up, bridging the gap between generations in a heartwarming way. Max realized that in the realm of cultural differences, authenticity was the key to connecting with customers.

By the end of the campaign, the revolutionary gadget had not only achieved impressive sales figures but had also become a symbol of unity between generations. Max's insightful approach to navigating cultural differences had turned what could have been a marketing disaster into a heartwarming success story.

In the grand tapestry of Max's marketing adventures, this chapter stood out as a shining example of how understanding and embracing cultural differences in customer behavior could lead to not only business success but also genuine connections that transcended borders and generations.

And so, Max added another feather to his cap, proving that in the realm of marketing, cultural sensitivity, a dash of humor, and a sprinkle of creativity could create stories that were both hilarious and heartwarming, while driving impactful results.

III

Challenges in Customer Understanding

Ahoy, Marketing Maestros! Picture this:
you've conquered countless campaigns,
authored tones of knowledge, and
enthralled audiences far and wide. Yet,
even the mightiest face challenges. In the
realm of Customer Understanding, the
maze of human behavior perplexes. Just as
a chameleon shifts hues, customers' desires
morph. Your expertise guides you, but the
dance of comprehension demands humor &
insight.

9

Chapter 9: Active Listening: A Key to Understanding Customers

O nce upon a time in the vibrant world of marketing, lived Marketer Max, a seasoned professional with more years of experience than he cared to count. Max was known for his witty one-liners, charismatic speeches, and a unique ability to turn even the most mundane marketing tasks into thrilling adventures.

One fine day, Max found himself facing a challenge that would put his skills to the ultimate test: understanding customers through active listening. Armed with his trusty notepad and a cup of coffee, Max set out on a journey that would forever change the way he approached his craft.

As Max dove into the realm of active listening, he

realized it was more than just nodding your head while pretending to care. It was an art that required genuine curiosity and an empathetic heart. To truly understand customers, he had to embark on a hilarious and insightful quest.

Chapter 9: The Misadventures of Max in Active Listening

In the bustling heart of the city, Max stumbled upon a small café. Intrigued by the melodious laughter echoing from within, he decided to step in. The café was a treasure trove of diverse individuals, each with their own stories and quirks.

Max spotted a group of friends engaged in animated conversation. He overheard snippets about their favorite products and brands. Eureka! Max realized this was the perfect opportunity to put his active listening skills to the test. He approached the group, armed with his notepad and a cheerful grin.

"Hey there, folks! Mind if I join your conversation? I'm Marketer Max, on a quest to understand customers like never before!" he exclaimed.

The group exchanged curious glances before bursting into laughter. "Sure, Max! We could use some entertainment," said Sarah, the resident comedian of the group.

As the conversation flowed, Max used his humor and charm to weave insightful questions seamlessly into the banter. "Tell me," he asked, leaning in with genuine curiosity, "what makes you choose one brand over another? Is it the catchy slogans or the unforgettable jingles?"

The friends exchanged amused looks before sharing their opinions. Max jotted down notes furiously, his excitement growing with each witty response. He learned that it wasn't just about slogans or jingles; it was about the emotional connection these elements created.

Max's adventure didn't stop there. He hopped from café to mall, engaging with shoppers, retail workers, and even the occasional confused tourist. Armed with his knack for storytelling, he transformed mundane conversations into riveting tales.

In a particularly memorable encounter, Max found himself chatting with an elderly lady who was shopping for her grandchildren. She shared stories of her past and the joy she found in spoiling her little ones. Max couldn't help but be touched by her sincerity and warmth. He realized that active listening wasn't just about extracting information; it was about connecting with people on a human level.

With a heart full of newfound wisdom and a notepad brimming with anecdotes, Max returned to his marketing realm. He crafted campaigns that resonated with the stories he had heard – the dreams, desires, and quirks of real people. And, true to his nature, he infused each campaign with a dash of humor that made customers smile.

In the end, Marketer Max had not only cracked the code of active listening but had also discovered a treasure trove of human stories that fueled his marketing endeavors. And so, dear readers, remember that active listening is not just a skill; it's a doorway to a world of laughter, insight, and connection.

And thus concludes Chapter 9: The Misadventures of Max in Active Listening. Stay tuned for more marketing escapades that will leave you chuckling and pondering the intricacies of this captivating realm!

10

Chapter 10: Asking the Right Questions to Discover Customer Needs

I n a world buzzing with marketing strategies and promotional tactics, there lies a secret weapon that can unlock the treasure trove of customer needs: the art of asking the right questions. Imagine this scenario: You walk into a bustling café, ready to meet a friend. As you sit down and chat, you realize that your friend seems to know an uncanny amount about your likes, dislikes, and preferences. How did they become a mind reader? The answer lies in their skillful interrogation!

As a seasoned marketer with over two decades of experience, you've come to understand that truly comprehending your customers' needs goes beyond mere surface-level interactions. It's about digging deeper, like an archaeologist on a mission to uncover the golden nuggets of information that can shape your marketing strategies.

The Quirky Questionnaire Quest:

Let's embark on a tale of John, a brilliant marketer whose unconventional approach to asking questions transformed his campaigns. John had a fascination with peculiar questions that not only grabbed attention but also unearthed valuable insights. Instead of the usual "What do you want?" John's questionnaire posed questions like "If your life was a movie, what would be its tagline?" or "If your business were an animal, what would it roar like?"

These unconventional questions acted like magic keys that unlocked the doors to customers' thoughts and emotions. They provoked deeper contemplation and provided insights that were not just informative, but downright hilarious at times. For instance, one respondent claimed his business would roar like a caffeinated squirrel on a mission – not the expected answer for an IT consultancy!

The Detective's Dive:

But asking offbeat questions wasn't the only trick up John's sleeve. He knew that the magic wasn't just in the questions, but in the art of active listening. Like a detective hot on the trail of a suspect, John honed his listening skills. He paid attention to the pauses, the sighs, and the moments when a customer's eyes sparkled with excitement.

In one memorable instance, John met a client who was interested in guerrilla marketing. The client mentioned a fascination with underground music venues and their mysterious aura. Instead of jumping into a sales pitch, John asked, "What if your brand could be the 'underground rockstar' of your industry?" The client's eyes lit up, and a partnership was born. All thanks to a dash of creativity and a sprinkle of empathetic listening.

The Oracle of Customer Whims:
As an author of over 103 books, you understand the power of storytelling. Similarly, the art of asking questions is a storytelling endeavor in itself. Each question is a chapter, each response a plot twist. The more you uncover, the richer your narrative becomes. In your consulting sessions on gamification, guerrilla marketing, and lead generation, you have witnessed firsthand how customers open up when they feel their voices are truly heard.

Remember, Marketer Max, every question you ask

is a bridge to a customer's heart. By delving beyond the surface, you can unveil desires that even your customers might not have fully realized themselves. Just as your quirky stories have captivated readers across your 103 books, your skillful questioning can captivate your audience's needs and transform your marketing endeavors into tales of success.

So, in the grand symphony of marketing, remember that the melody of questions can be both hilarious and insightful, leading you to the crescendo of customer satisfaction. Just like your stories, the art of questioning weaves a tapestry of connection, engagement, and ultimately, triumph.

With your expert certification in hand and your curiosity as your compass, embark on this journey of discovery. The next time you sit across from a client or stand on stage as an orator, remember that the right question can unravel the enigma of customer needs, making you not just an influencer, but a true magician of marketing insight.

11

Chapter 11: Empathy: Connecting on a Deeper Level

Once upon a time in the bustling city of Marketingville, there lived a legendary marketer named Max. Max was known far and wide for his exceptional skills in gamification, guerrilla marketing, and lead generation. He had a reputation for turning even the most mundane products into viral sensations. However, there was one secret weapon in Max's arsenal that set him apart from the rest: his unparalleled ability to connect with people on a deeper level through empathy.

Max firmly believed that marketing wasn't just about selling products; it was about forging genuine connections with customers. He often reminisced about a particular campaign that showcased his mastery of empathy.

One day, Max was approached by a small, family-run bakery struggling to compete with larger chains in the city. The bakery owners poured their hearts and souls into their delectable treats, but their sales were crumbling like stale cookies. Max knew he had to dive deep into empathy to crack this crusty challenge.

He began by immersing himself in the bakery's world. He spent time kneading dough, frosting cupcakes, and listening to the owners' stories. He learned about their family traditions, the grand-mother's secret recipes, and the memories woven into each creation. Max realized that the bakery's true magic wasn't just in the taste of the pastries but in the love that went into making them.

Inspired by this insight, Max crafted a campaign that tugged at heartstrings and taste buds alike. He created a video that showcased the bakery's history, complete with black-and-white photos of the founders rolling dough alongside heartwarming anecdotes. The video wasn't just about the food; it was about the legacy, the passion, and the emotions baked into every product.

Max's campaign spread like wildfire across social media. People shared the video with tearful emojis and nostalgic comments. The story resonated with individuals who had their own cherished family recipes and traditions. The campaign wasn't just about promoting the bakery; it was about celebrating the essence of family and connection.

Within weeks, the bakery experienced a surge in foot traffic and online orders. Customers weren't just buying pastries; they were buying into the bakery's story and becoming a part of its extended family. Max's empathetic approach had turned a struggling business into a local sensation.

As Max reflected on this triumph, he realized that empathy was the secret ingredient that every marketer needed. Understanding the hopes, dreams, and pain points of customers allowed him to create campaigns that genuinely touched their hearts. Max's journey through Marketingville had taught him that connection was the key to unlocking success.

And so, dear readers, remember that in the world of marketing, empathy is your most potent tool. Just like Max, put yourself in your customers' shoes, feel their joys and struggles, and craft campaigns that resonate on a human level. Because in the end, it's not just about selling products; it's about creating stories that people will cherish and share for generations to come.

12

Chapter 12: Building Rapport for Improved Customer Understanding

O nce upon a time, in the enchanted realm of Marketingville, lived a savvy marketer named Max. Max was renowned not only for his expertise in crafting catchy campaigns but also for his uncanny ability to build connections with customers that transcended the ordinary.

In the digital age, where emojis ruled and "LOL" became the universal language, Max knew that forming a real connection with customers required more than just witty one-liners. It was about establishing a rapport that felt like sharing a cup of virtual coffee while discussing the latest trends.

Picture this: Max was working on a campaign for a quirky startup that sold customizable sneakers.

The challenge was getting to know their diverse customer base. Instead of relying solely on data analytics, Max had a brilliant idea. He decided to throw a "Sneaker Stories" contest on Instagram, encouraging customers to share the tales behind their favorite kicks.

Stories flooded in from every corner of the globe. Max was moved by a touching entry from a customer in Tokyo who used their sneakers to complete their first marathon. Another entrant from Brazil had a pair that had been through countless music festivals, each scuff telling a different melody.

Max took these stories and weaved them into a heartwarming campaign that resonated deeply. The sneakers were no longer just products; they were companions on life's journey. Customers felt understood, as if Max had unlocked their personal archives.

But the magic didn't stop there. Max saw an opportunity to take rapport-building to the next level. He organized a virtual Sneaker Soiree where customers could join a live online event. The highlight? A "Sneaker Confession Booth" where attendees shared their quirkiest sneaker-related secrets.

During the soiree, Max shared his own tale of mistakenly wearing mismatched sneakers to a major presentation. The laughter that ensued created an atmosphere of camaraderie. Customers realized that even the marketing maestro himself had stumbled over his shoelaces once in a while.

The event wasn't just insightful; it was downright hilarious. The CEO of the startup confessed that he had a secret stash of superhero-themed sneakers hidden in his office, sparking a trend among the attendees to share their own quirky collections.

Max's ingenious approach not only boosted customer engagement but also provided the startup with invaluable insights. They learned that their sneakers weren't just products; they were tokens of personal stories, expressions of identity, and catalysts for conversations.

As Max wrapped up the chapter on "Unleashing Rapport Magic," he reflected on the power of connection. In a world where data-driven algorithms often dictated marketing decisions, he proved that human stories and shared laughter could transform customers into loyal advocates.

And so, the tale of Max, the marketer who turned

customers into BFFs, became a legend in Market-ingville. His approach was a reminder that behind every transaction was a human heart waiting to be touched. And the next time you lace up your sneakers, remember the stories they hold – you might just find yourself sharing a laugh with a kindred spirit halfway across the world.

IV

Techniques to Help Customers Discover What They Want

Once upon a time in the vibrant realm of marketing, Marketer Max donned his creative cape to unravel the enigma of customer desires. With 2 decades of wisdom, he crafted a symphony of techniques. From gamification that turned product exploration into a thrilling quest, to guerrilla tactics that whispered secrets in unexpected places. With his mastery in lead generation, Max danced through the digital maze, armed with HubSpot's magic wand and Digital Vidya's spells.

13

Chapter 13: Guiding Customers Through the Exploration Phase

I n the mystical realm of marketing, where ideas dance like fireflies in the night, our protagonist, Marketer Max, embarks on a quest to unravel the secrets of guiding customers through the treacherous terrain known as the Exploration Phase. Armed with a sword made of wit and a shield forged from insight, Max sets out on a hilarious and enlightening journey.

Section 1: The Enigmatic Call

In the bustling market square, Max encounters a group of curious souls. They're like lost adventurers, standing at the crossroads of indecision. Armed with their smartphones, they are eager to explore the uncharted territories of products and services.

Max, with a twinkle in his eye, approaches them and shares a tale of a time when he himself was a bewildered wanderer in the vast sea of choices.

"Once upon a time, I was a young marketing squire, venturing into the world of exotic offerings. I stumbled upon a peculiar artifact called 'The Widget of Whimsy.' Its dazzling features bewildered me, and I knew I had to learn more. But alas, the Exploration Phase was a labyrinthine riddle! With every twist and turn, I found myself ensnared in a web of conflicting reviews, intricate specifications, and an abundance of jargon.

But fear not, for I, too, found my guiding star. I discovered the power of storytelling. I crafted a tale around the Widget of Whimsy, painting a picture of how it would transform lives and bring joy to even the grumpiest of gnomes. And lo and behold, my fellow explorers were entranced by my tale, eager to dive into the enchanting world of the widget. The Exploration Phase became a magical dance of imagination and curiosity."

Section 2: The Map of Empathy

Max's expedition takes him to a hidden oasis where a wise sage imparts a profound lesson. With a hearty laugh, Max recounts the sage's wisdom:

"Ah, my friends, the Exploration Phase is like a labyrinthine garden of curiosity. To navigate its twists and turns, you must wield the Map of Empathy. Place yourself in the shoes of these brave explorers. Understand their desires, their fears, and their dreams. Create content that speaks directly to their hearts, addressing their questions and quelling their doubts. For when you guide them through this maze with the torch of empathy, you become their beacon of trust."

Section 3: The Potion of Engagement

Onward Max goes, encountering a mischievous sprite known as 'The Distractor.' This cheeky creature thrives on sidetracking explorers from their path. Max, with a wink and a chuckle, shares his secret weapon:

"Aha! The Potion of Engagement, my dear companions! Just as a master storyteller weaves a tale that keeps listeners at the edge of their seats, so must you craft content that captivates the wandering minds of your audience. Combine the essence of humor, curiosity, and surprise to concoct a potion that enchants their senses. With every sip, they'll be drawn deeper into your narrative, safely navigating the Exploration Phase without succumbing to the mischievous distractions."

Section 4: The Treasure of Clarity

As Max's expedition nears its end, he stumbles upon a hidden trove known as 'The Treasure of Clarity.' With a hearty guffaw, Max unravels its secrets:

"Ah, my fellow wayfarers, the Exploration Phase need not be a puzzle shrouded in darkness. No, no! Illuminate the path with the torch of clarity. Provide your explorers with clear signposts, easy-to-understand information, and a roadmap that guides them towards their destination. The more you simplify and demystify, the more confidently they will tread, and the more likely they'll emerge from the Exploration Phase as loyal companions on your journey."

And so, Marketer Max's hilarious and insightful expedition through the Exploration Phase comes to an end. As he stands atop the hill, overlooking the vast landscape of consumer curiosity, he chuckles heartily, knowing that armed with empathy, engagement, and clarity, he can guide any intrepid explorer through the labyrinth of choices, turning them into loyal comrades on the grand adventure of marketing.

And thus, dear readers, may you too find your way through the whimsical wilderness of the Exploration Phase, armed with Max's sage advice and a hearty dose of laughter.

Chapter 14: Using Customer Stories as a Discovery Tool

I n the world of marketing, where every tactic and strategy vies for attention, there's a gem hidden in plain sight – the captivating and awe-inspiring world of customer stories. Now, hold onto your marketing hats, my fellow adventurers, as we delve into Chapter 14 of our marketing odyssey: "Using Customer Stories as a Discovery Tool."

Picture this: you're sitting by a cozy fireplace, sipping a cup of coffee, when your email pings. You open it, and voilà! It's a heartfelt testimonial from a customer who not only loves your product but has also had their life transformed by it. Now, what do you do? You don't just read it and smile (although that's a great start). You, my dear marketer, use this goldmine of a customer story as a powerful discovery tool.

Let's step into the shoes of Jane, an ingenious marketer, who transformed her entire campaign using a single customer story.

The Tale of Transformation: Jane's Journey

Jane had always been fascinated by the emotional resonance of stories. So, when she stumbled upon a heartfelt email from a customer named Sarah, she knew she struck marketing gold. Sarah's story was nothing short of magic – she had been struggling with productivity until she found Jane's time management app. Sarah's heartfelt account of how the app turned her from a procrastinator into a productivity wizard was awe-inspiring.

With a spark in her eyes, Jane didn't just send a thank-you note to Sarah. She knew that this story could be the key to unlocking new dimensions of her marketing strategy. She crafted a full-fledged campaign around Sarah's journey, turning it into an adventure of transformation.

The Five Acts of Customer Story Magic

Act 1: Elicit Emotions

Jane's campaign began with a bang – she shared Sarah's story across social media platforms. The power of Sarah's transformation resonated with others who faced similar challenges. People were drawn to the authenticity of the story, connecting on a deeper level.

Act 2: The Hero's Journey
Sarah wasn't just a satisfied customer; she was the hero of her own journey. Jane used this narrative structure to unfold Sarah's struggle, her encounter with the app, and the ultimate triumph over her productivity demons. The audience was captivated, rooting for Sarah every step of the way.

Act 3: Relatable Challenges
Jane used Sarah's story to address common pain points faced by her target audience. She cleverly showed how Sarah's struggles mirrored their own, creating a sense of camaraderie and empathy.

Act 4: Transformative Solutions
Just as the hero discovers the magic sword, Sarah found the app. Jane showcased the app's features and benefits, turning it into the hero's tool for transformation. The audience could now visualize themselves wielding the same power.

Act 5: Call to Action

The climax arrived when Jane invited the audience to take action – to experience their own transformation through the app. The response was overwhelming as people lined up to be part of the journey.

The Result: A Marketing Symphony

Jane's campaign, inspired by Sarah's story, hit all the right notes. Engagement skyrocketed, sales surged, and testimonials poured in. But the true magic lay in the connection forged between Jane's brand and her audience. Through a single customer story, Jane had uncovered a treasure trove of discovery.

And so, my fellow marketers, as you venture forth into the realm of customer stories, remember that these tales are not just words on a screen; they are portals to emotions, empathy, and transformation. Harness the power of stories, and you'll discover a marketing adventure like no other. And who knows, maybe one day, your own marketing tale will be the one that inspires others to journey onward.

So there you have it, Chapter 14: "Using Customer Stories as a Discovery Tool," filled with the enchanting journey of Jane, the marketer who found her muse in a single customer's story. Now, go forth, my fellow marketers, and weave your own marketing symphony using the threads of customer stories!

15

Chapter 15: Presenting Options: Helping Customers Make Informed Choices

O nce upon a time in the bustling city of Marketville, there lived a seasoned marketer named Max. Max had spent decades mastering the art of marketing, filling the shelves of Amazon with more books than one could count, and captivating audiences with his charismatic orations on various platforms. His expertise was not just limited to marketing; he had honed his skills in the realms of gamification, guerrilla marketing, and lead generation, making him a true guru in the world of business.

One sunny morning, Max found himself in an enchanting coffee shop called "Choice Brews," known for its aromatic blends and vibrant atmosphere. As he sipped his favorite brew, he couldn't help but notice the flurry of activity around him. People were browsing through a myriad of coffee options, each presented with its unique flavor profile, origin story, and brewing method. The coffee barista, a cheerful individual named Lily, was skillfully guiding customers through their choices.

Intrigued by Lily's approach, Max struck up a conversation. "You seem to have mastered the art of helping customers make choices," he said with a chuckle.

Lily grinned and replied, "Well, it's all about understanding their preferences and presenting options that align with their tastes. Just like in marketing, you know!"

Max's eyes sparkled with curiosity. "Tell me more. How do you present options in a way that helps customers make informed decisions?"

Lily leaned in and shared her wisdom. "Think of it as a storytelling experience. Each coffee has its unique journey – from the coffee farms nestled in the highlands to the roasting process that brings out its distinct flavors. I weave these stories into the options I present. For instance, if someone loves adventurous flavors, I'd tell them about our 'Jungle Expedition' blend, taking them on a taste adventure through the wilds of coffee beans."

Max nodded in appreciation. "Ah, so it's about personalization and connection."

"Exactly!" Lily exclaimed. "And just like you do in your marketing, I highlight the features that resonate with the customer. For someone looking for a caffeine kick, I'd talk about the high caffeine content of our 'Energetic Sunrise' blend. It's about addressing their needs."

Max scribbled a note in his notebook, his eyes gleaming with inspiration. "And how about over-whelming choices?"

Lily chuckled knowingly. "Too many options can be confusing, just like a cluttered marketing message. I limit the options based on what they're looking for – light, medium, or dark roast. It streamlines the decision-making process."

As they chatted, Max's mind raced with ideas. He thought back to his experiences in consulting on gamification and guerrilla marketing. Just as Lily used storytelling and personalization to guide coffee enthusiasts, he realized he could do the same with his clients. He could create engaging narratives around different marketing strategies, tailor them to the client's unique needs, and simplify the options to prevent decision paralysis.

After bidding Lily farewell and leaving the coffee shop, Max couldn't wait to put his newfound insights into practice. With a heart full of inspiration, he knew that just as Lily had helped customers find their perfect cup of coffee, he would help his clients find their perfect marketing blend – one that would leave a lasting impression on their audience.

And so, armed with the power of storytelling, personalization, and simplicity, Max continued his journey as a marketer, bringing his clients' visions to life and helping them make informed choices that would lead to success stories of their own. Just as he had learned from Lily at "Choice Brews," the art of presenting options was not just about business; it was about creating meaningful connections and guiding others toward their desired destinations.

16

Chapter 16: Providing a Personalized Customer Experience

O nce upon a time in the bustling world of marketing, there lived a seasoned marketer named Max. Max had seen marketing evolve over the decades, from the days of snail mail to the era of social media and beyond. But there was one principle that had remained constant throughout his journey: the power of providing a personalized customer experience.

Picture this: Max was invited to speak at a prestigious marketing conference in a glamorous city. As he stood on the stage, the spotlight highlighting his confident grin, he began to regale the audience with a tale that perfectly captured the essence of personalized customer experiences.

"Imagine," Max began, "that you're strolling through a quaint bookstore. You find yourself browsing through the shelves, seeking that one book that speaks directly to your soul. Just as you're about to give up, a friendly store assistant approaches with a warm smile."

Max's audience leaned in, captivated by his story-telling prowess.

"The assistant says, 'I noticed you're drawn to mystery novels. Have you checked out this new release? It's a tantalizing blend of suspense and wit, just like the stories you seem to enjoy.'"

He paused for effect, letting the anticipation build.

"As you take the book in your hands, you notice a personalized note slipped between its pages. It's from the author, expressing gratitude for your interest and including a recommendation for a nearby café known for its cozy atmosphere—a place where you can immerse yourself in the world of the book."

The audience chuckled, envisioning themselves in the story.

"Isn't that magical?" Max exclaimed. "This is

the heart of providing a personalized customer experience. It's about knowing your customers intimately, understanding their preferences, and delivering experiences that resonate with them on a personal level."

Max continued, recounting his own experiences in the world of marketing. "I once consulted with a small business owner who ran a gourmet bakery. She had a loyal customer named Emily who adored cupcakes. Not just any cupcakes, but those with a touch of lavender. Armed with this knowledge, the bakery owner surprised Emily with a box of freshly baked lavender-infused cupcakes on her birthday. Emily was over the moon and shared her delight on social media, spreading the word about the bakery's exceptional personalized touch."

The audience was enthralled, chuckles and nods of agreement echoing through the room.

"Think of personalization as a symphony," Max mused. "Each note is tailored to the listener's ear, creating a harmonious experience that lingers long after the last chord. And technology? It's the conductor's baton, orchestrating data insights and customer interactions to compose the perfect melody of engagement."

Max shared another tale, this time from his own writing journey. "In my life as an author, I've learned that personalized marketing extends beyond products and services. I once sent a signed copy of my latest book to a devoted reader who had just celebrated a milestone birthday. The reader was elated, not just because of the book, but because I had taken the time to acknowledge their special day. That connection transformed a reader into a lifelong fan."

He concluded with a hearty laugh, "So, my fellow marketers, let's remember that personalized customer experiences aren't just a strategy—they're an art form. Embrace the knowledge you have about your customers, and weave it into a tapestry of delight. Just like the assistant in the bookstore, let's help our customers find the stories they're looking for, and leave them with a heartfelt note that says, 'You matter.'"

The room erupted in applause as Max took his final bow, leaving behind a trail of inspiration and laughter.

And so, dear readers, remember Max's tale as you venture into the world of marketing. Craft your personalized symphony, sprinkle it with genuine care, and watch as your customers dance to the tune of unforgettable experiences.

V

Solving the Customer Dilemma

Marketer Max, the seasoned guru of all things marketing, unveils his latest masterpiece, "Solving the Customer Dilemma: What They Want." With over two decades of expertise, Max dives deep into the labyrinth of consumer desires, unraveling mysteries with a dash of humor. Through 103 books on Amazon and a legion of followers on Quora, LinkedIn, and Instagram, Max's insights are akin to golden nuggets. Step into Max's world and witness how even the trickiest riddles of customer desires.

17

Chapter 17: Analyzing Customer Pain Points and Providing Solutions

In the world of marketing, understanding your audience isn't just about knowing their preferences and desires; it's about diving deep into their woes and emerging as their problem-solving superhero. Our journey through the realms of marketing has brought us to a pivotal juncture: the art of analyzing customer pain points and crafting ingenious solutions. So, buckle up, fellow marketers, as we embark on this exhilarating quest for turning frowns into resounding applause.

Section 1: Peeling the Layers of Customer Discontent

"Once upon a time, in a land filled with products and services, lived a horde of unsatisfied customers with tales of woe..."

Here we delve into the heart of the matter, where we unearth the pain points that irk our customers. It's like being a detective in a mystery novel, except the mystery is what's causing those furrowed brows and exasperated sighs. Through anecdotes and real-life examples, we'll uncover the underlying motivations behind customer dissatisfaction. Remember, every grimace is an opportunity waiting to be seized!

Section 2: Empathy as Your Superpower

"Picture yourself in your customer's shoes: uncomfortably tight, slightly worn out, yet carrying the weight of dreams and expectations."

Empathy is the cornerstone of our success in resolving customer pain points. We'll explore how to channel our inner empath to forge connections that bridge the gap between us and them. Through side-splitting stories of misunderstandings and "Oops, we did it again" moments, we'll grasp the essence of being in sync with our audience's emotions.

Section 3: The Art of Solution Crafting

"When life gives you lemons, make a sour-faced

customer into a lemonade enthusiast."

This is where the magic happens. Armed with the insights we've gathered, we'll venture into the realm of solution crafting. We'll walk the fine line between innovation and practicality, and spin tales of how legendary marketers turned customer pain points into opportunities for growth. From designing personalized experiences to creating products that mend broken hearts, we'll master the art of solution alchemy.

Section 4: The Hero's Journey - Marketing Edition

"With a cape of creativity and a sword of strategy, our hero ventured forth to conquer the formidable mountain of customer dissatisfaction."

In this chapter's thrilling climax, we'll witness the epic tales of marketers who dared to challenge the norm and emerged victorious. Their sagas of courage, wit, and unyielding determination will inspire us to tackle even the most perplexing pain points head-on. Through their stories, we'll learn that failure is just a stepping stone on the path to innovation.

Section 5: The Joy of Triumph

"And so, after much toil, sweat, and probably a few sleepless nights, our marketer emerged from the battlefield triumphant."

In the final section, we'll bask in the glow of success stories that transformed customer dissatisfaction into loyalty and adoration. Through anecdotes of customers turned brand advocates, we'll relish the fruits of our labor and celebrate the power of turning pain points into triumphs.

So, my fellow marketing adventurers, let's don our capes of creativity, wield our swords of strategy, and embark on this journey to transform customer pain points into stepping stones toward success. With wit, empathy, and a touch of marketing magic, we'll conquer even the most elusive of customer woes and emerge as champions of innovation. Onward, to a world where every problem becomes a possibility!

18

Chapter 18: Handling Customer Confusion with Clarity

In the realm of marketing, my dear reader, there exists a phenomenon as curious as it is perplexing: the bewildering dance of customer confusion. Picture this: a potential customer is browsing through your website, eyes darting from product to product, like a bee buzzing through a garden of possibilities. They're intrigued, but alas, a cloud of uncertainty descends upon them. The labyrinth of options, the jargon-laden descriptions, the perplexing pricing tiers – it's as if they've stumbled into a cryptic crossword puzzle!

But fret not, for in this chapter, we shall embark on a quest to conquer confusion and illuminate the path to clarity. Imagine we're entering the mystical land of "Clarusia," where befuddled customers roam and marketers wield the wands of simplicity.

Scene 1: The Enchanted Maze of Jargon

Once upon a time in Clarusia, there lived a humble merchant named Marcus, who sold revolutionary gadgets known as "Wondroblasters." Marcus was armed with a treasure trove of technical knowledge, which he inadvertently wielded like a double-edged sword. As customers approached his stall, his eyes twinkled with eagerness to educate. However, instead of marveling at the Wondroblasters, customers gaped in befuddlement at his jargon-laden explanations.

In this tale, dear reader, Marcus learned a valuable lesson: speaking in tongues only understood by tech wizards is akin to casting a spell of confusion upon unsuspecting customers. He transformed his explanations into enchanting stories of how the Wondroblasters simplified lives, leaving behind baffling acronyms in favor of relatable anecdotes.

Scene 2: The Tower of Pricing Perplexity

In the heart of Clarusia, stood the Tower of Pricing Perplexity – a structure so tall that it tickled the clouds. It was inhabited by the Price Goblin, who loved nothing more than scattering pricing tiers like confetti. Once, a brave adventurer named Ava approached the tower, seeking the magical "SimpliDeal" potion. The potion was said to banish confusion and reveal the perfect pricing plan.

The Price Goblin cackled and presented Ava with a table of twenty-six pricing options, each with its own set of fine print. Ava's eyebrows furrowed, and she felt a shiver of confusion crawl up her spine. In that moment of despair, she recalled an ancient proverb: "When in doubt, seek clarity."

Ava harnessed her courage and requested a meeting with the Tower's architect. With a wave of his wand, the architect condensed the pricing tiers into three simple options, each adorned with the benefits they bestowed. Ava left the tower with the SimpliDeal potion, her heart lightened by the newfound clarity.

Scene 3: The Oracle of User-Friendly UI

At the crossroads of Clarusia, where digital pathways converged, stood the Oracle of User-Friendly UI. She possessed the uncanny ability to foresee where customers would stumble and fall in the labyrinth of a website. One day, Mark, a passionate entrepreneur, sought her wisdom.

"Oracle," Mark implored, "how do I vanquish the confusion that lurks within my website?"

The Oracle smiled knowingly and guided Mark through a vision of simplicity. She showed him a world where buttons were bold and beckoning, navigation was intuitive as a babbling brook, and the checkout process flowed like a symphony. Mark returned to reality, his mind brimming with insights.

Armed with the Oracle's guidance, Mark transformed his website into a user-friendly oasis. Customers rejoiced, their confusion swept away by the gentle winds of clarity, and Mark's sales flourished like never before.

And so, dear reader, as we conclude this chapter in the Clarity Chronicles, let us remember that handling customer confusion with clarity is a noble quest, filled with enchanting tales and valuable lessons. Just as Marcus, Ava, and Mark discovered, simplicity is the elixir that transforms bewilderment into bliss, ensuring that customers tread the path of enlightenment rather than the maze of mystification.

Chapter 19: Managing Expectations: Setting Realistic Goals

O nce upon a time in the bustling world of marketing, our protagonist, Marketer Max, found himself in a peculiar situation. He had just taken on a new project with a client who had wild, ambitious dreams of skyrocketing sales and achieving overnight fame. The client, let's call them Enthusiastic Ellie, was convinced that a single marketing campaign could turn their startup into the next unicorn.

Max knew he had his work cut out for him. He had seen this scenario play out countless times in his two decades of experience. Enthusiasm was great, but it needed a dose of reality. Max realized that it was his responsibility to manage expectations and set achievable goals.

As Max sat down with Ellie for a strategy session, he began by recounting a humorous anecdote. He shared the story of a time he tried to bake a cake without any prior experience. With grand visions of a towering confection, he threw in all sorts of ingredients without measuring, and the result was a culinary catastrophe. The cake collapsed, just like overly ambitious marketing plans often did.

Chuckling, Max segued into the heart of the matter. He explained to Ellie that setting goals in marketing was much like baking a cake. You needed the right ingredients, proper measurements, and patience to let it all come together.

Max illustrated the concept using a story about a friend who wanted to run a marathon. Rather than expecting to run 26 miles right away, his friend followed a training plan, starting with shorter distances and gradually building up endurance. It was a journey, not a sprint. Similarly, Max emphasized that marketing success required a step-by-step approach.

Drawing inspiration from his bookshelf adorned with his 103 Amazon bestsellers, Max provided Ellie with a checklist of how to set realistic marketing goals:

Know Thyself: Just as a marathon runner needs to assess their current fitness level, a business must understand its starting point. Analyze past performance, market trends, and competition before charting a course.

Break It Down: Aiming for the stars is admirable, but breaking the journey into smaller, achievable milestones is more effective. Max shared a witty analogy of how even climbing Mount Everest is done in stages, each camp becoming a stepping stone to the summit.

Data Detective: Max recalled a detective story from his own marketing adventures. By tracking data, he once uncovered a hidden treasure trove of insights that guided a campaign back on track. Ellie was intrigued by the idea of data-driven decision-making.

Reality Check-In: Just as a GPS adjusts the route based on real-time traffic, marketing plans need periodic reality checks. Max recounted a humorous tale of a GPS directing him to drive into a lake. He narrowly avoided disaster by trusting his instincts—a lesson in being adaptable.

Celebrate the Victories: Max shared a heartwarming story of a team celebrating each milestone reached during a campaign. From small wins to big achievements, recognizing progress boosted morale and kept the momentum alive.

By the end of their conversation, Max and Ellie were both laughing and enlightened. Ellie realized that while dreams were essential, they needed to be grounded in reality. Max's knack for weaving stories and real-life examples made the concept of managing expectations and setting realistic goals a memorable and impactful lesson.

And so, armed with a newfound appreciation for the art of goal-setting, Max and Ellie embarked on their marketing journey—one that balanced ambition with a healthy dose of practicality. After all, even the most epic sagas start with a single, well-considered step.

20

Chapter 20: Turning Dissatisfaction into Loyalty

O nce upon a time in the bustling city of Marketingville, there lived a seasoned marketer named Max. Max was known far and wide for his ingenious marketing strategies and his ability to turn even the most dissatisfied customers into loyal brand advocates. It was a skill he had honed over the years, and it was time to unveil his secrets to the world.

The Curious Case of Clara's Coffee Catastrophe

In a cozy corner of Marketingville, there was a charming little coffee shop called "Clara's Coffee Haven." Clara, the owner, had built a loyal following of caffeine enthusiasts. But one gloomy day, disaster struck. The espresso machine decided to take an unscheduled coffee break, leaving a line of frustrated customers and a jittery staff in its wake.

Clara was at her wit's end when Max walked in, sensing an opportunity. He ordered his usual cappuccino and struck up a conversation with Clara. She poured out her woes, and Max listened intently, his marketing gears already turning.

"Clara," Max began with a twinkle in his eye, "remember that time when the famous writer J.K. Roastling visited your coffee shop? Why not turn this espresso emergency into a legendary tale? Let's call it 'The Great Espresso Exodus.'"

Max's plan was set in motion. He created quirky posters and social media teasers about the "Espresso Exodus," complete with dramatic graphics of the espresso machine dressed as an adventurer exploring the coffee bean jungles. The coffee shop buzzed with excitement as customers shared the hilarious campaign.

Brewing Loyalty, One Cup at a Time
As the days rolled on, Clara's Coffee Haven transformed into a hub of laughter and stories. Customers eagerly shared their own "espresso exodus" tales while sipping on freshly brewed cups. The wait for the espresso machine's return turned into a

shared journey of anticipation, and the frustration of that initial day melted away.

Max didn't stop there. He collaborated with Clara to offer surprise discounts to customers who shared their own creative coffee adventure stories on social media. He even organized a "Welcome Back Espresso" party, where the repaired machine was paraded through the café like a returning hero.

The Espresso Effect: From Dissatisfaction to Devotion

What happened next was pure magic. Not only did Clara's Coffee Haven regain its usual flow of customers, but it actually saw an increase in foot traffic. The "Espresso Exodus" had turned into an unexpected brand-building saga that resonated with both regulars and newcomers.

Clara's coffee shop had turned dissatisfaction into an opportunity for connection. Max's unique approach had transformed disgruntled customers into brand evangelists. People shared their stories of how a seemingly negative experience had turned into a positive memory. The power of storytelling and humor had created an unbreakable bond between the coffee shop and its patrons.

Lessons Learned

Empathy is Key: Max's success in this situation began with his ability to empathize with Clara's frustration. Understanding the pain points of your customers is the first step in crafting a solution that truly resonates.

Storytelling and Humor: By turning the coffee machine mishap into a playful adventure, Max engaged customers on an emotional level. People remember stories that make them smile and laugh, and these memories foster stronger connections.

Inclusive Engagement: Max encouraged customer participation in the campaign, making them co-creators of the brand experience. Involving customers in your marketing efforts not only builds loyalty but also sparks creativity and engagement.

Seizing Opportunities: Every challenge presents an opportunity. Max didn't just fix the espresso machine; he turned the situation into a remarkable story that boosted brand loyalty.

So, dear readers, remember the tale of Clara's Coffee Haven and the Espresso Exodus. The next time dissatisfaction knocks on your door, don't just chase it away – invite it in for a cup of creativity and watch how it can transform into the most loyal of allies. After all, turning sour situations into sweet victories is the true essence of masterful marketing, as Marketer Max well knew.

VI

Strategies for Enhancing Customer Understanding

Ahoy, Marketer Extraordinaire! 🔋🐎
Looking to unravel the enigma of customer desires? "Strategies for Enhancing Customer Understanding: Decoding Desires 101" is your treasure map! Just like crafting the perfect marketing campaign, this guide navigates through the labyrinth of customer preferences. With insights as sharp as a finely honed pitch, it's like reading your audience's minds – but without the psychic hotline bills! Get ready to decode desires and turn heads with your newfound marketing

21

Chapter 21: Leveraging Technology to Understand Customer Preferences

Once upon a time, in the bustling world of marketing, there lived Marketer Max, a seasoned guru with a penchant for both the old-school charm of handshakes and the futuristic allure of high-tech gadgets. He had seen trends come and go like fashion fads, but one thing remained constant: the importance of understanding customer preferences. With a twinkle in his eye and a keyboard at his fingertips, Marketer Max set out to explore the wild world of leveraging technology to truly know what made customers tick.

The Techno-Quest Begins

In the land of pixels and codes, Marketer Max embarked on his journey to harness technology for decoding the enigmatic preferences of his target audience. Armed with his trusty tablet and a healthy dose of curiosity, he delved into the world of data analytics. Through the labyrinthine paths of spread-sheets and graphs, he began to unveil patterns that were once hidden in the shadows.

The Enchanted Algorithms

Amidst the digital forest of algorithms, Max stumbled upon the Algorithm of Taste Buds. This magical formula could predict with uncanny accuracy whether a customer preferred pineap-ple on their pizza or considered it a culinary abomination. Max chuckled at the absurdity, but he realized that such insights could shape powerful marketing campaigns. Armed with this knowledge, he launched a pizza parlor campaign that divided the city between #TeamPineapple and #TeamNoPineapple. The debate reached such fervor that even the mayor declared their allegiance! All this from decoding food preferences - truly a slice of success!

Virtual Reality Revelations

But Marketer Max wasn't content with just knowing taste buds. He donned his virtual reality headset and plunged into a world where customers' deepest desires were laid bare. In this realm, he witnessed firsthand the dreams and aspirations of his audience. He saw Jane, a young aspiring astronaut, yearning for a taste of zero gravity. Max grinned, seeing the opportunity. He partnered with a local amusement park to create a simulated space adventure. The campaign not only thrilled Jane but also launched Max's brand into the stratosphere of creativity.

The Chatbot Chronicles

Ah, the chatbots! Those digital minions who tirelessly answered customer queries day and night. Marketer Max, being the humorous soul he was, decided to infuse a dash of personality into these bots. He programmed them with witty responses that left customers in splits. One day, a confused customer asked the chatbot for the meaning of life. Without missing a beat, the bot replied, "To find out why customers like you ask such deep questions, of course!" The screenshot of that exchange went viral, and suddenly, Max's brand was associated with both humor and efficiency.

A Lesson in Data Privacy

But Max's technological exploits came with their own set of challenges. He learned the hard way that his data-gathering tactics needed to respect the boundaries of privacy. In a tale of irony, his campaign on personalized toothbrushes led to whispers of "Big Brother" surveillance. Max swiftly corrected his course, showing the world that he wasn't just a marketer but a responsible steward of customer trust.

The Grand Finale

As the sun set on Marketer Max's tech-infused odyssey, he realized that the magic of understanding customer preferences wasn't just about data points and algorithms. It was about weaving a tapestry of connection between his brand and the people he served. By leveraging technology, Max had danced his way into the hearts and minds of his audience.

And so, dear readers, as we close this chapter, remember that technology is but a tool — it's the marketer's touch that transforms it into an unforgettable symphony of customer delight. So go forth, armed with your gadgets and gizmos, and may your tech tango be as enchanting as Marketer Max's.

Chapter 22: Data-Driven Insights: Using Analytics to Anticipate Needs

O nce upon a time in the realm of marketing wizardry, where metrics danced, graphs pirouetted, and spreadsheets sang melodious symphonies, lived Marketer Max. Max wasn't just any marketer; he was the maestro of data, the guru of analytics, and the oracle of anticipation. Armed with his trusty spreadsheet wand and a crystal ball made of pie charts, he embarked on a journey to uncover the enchanting secrets of data-driven insights.

The Spark of Curiosity

It all began on a sunny morning when Max stumbled upon a peculiar trend while analyzing the sales data for his latest book, "The Guerrilla Gamification Guide." The sales graph resembled a roller coaster, with sharp dips and exhilarating climbs. Chuckling to himself, he thought, "Ah, the sales numbers are riding their own thrill ride!"

But curiosity gripped him like a mischievous imp. He delved deeper, slicing and dicing the data like a culinary artist preparing a gourmet feast. As he sorted through the numbers, a pattern emerged. The sales dipped after a spike whenever he posted on LinkedIn, and they soared when he posted on Quora. Max's laughter echoed through his study as he realized that his LinkedIn posts seemed to have a peculiar knack for summoning a sales slump.

The Quest for Answers

Max embarked on his quest to decipher this mystical riddle. Armed with a notepad, a quill, and a magnifying glass, he began investigating the root of the conundrum. After a series of experiments and late-night espresso-fueled brainstorming sessions, he stumbled upon a whimsical insight.

Max realized that his LinkedIn posts were full of marketing jargon and industry buzzwords, sending potential readers into a befuddled slumber. On the other hand, his Quora posts were charming tales of marketing adventures, complete with dragons

106

of doubt and knights of creativity. The readers resonated with the stories, and thus, the sales soared like a phoenix from the ashes.

The Crystal Ball of Anticipation

Armed with this newfound knowledge, Max concocted a devious plan to transform his LinkedIn posts into enchanting stories. He traded his jargon-laden paragraphs for whimsical narratives, weaving magic and marketing into the same fabric. His next LinkedIn post read like a fairy tale: "Once upon a time, in the kingdom of ROI, a brave marketer embarked on a quest to conquer the elusive Conversion Dragon..."

The response was unprecedented. Comments flooded in with laughter and agreement, and the post went viral faster than a fireball spell. Sales spiked, and Max's book soared to the top of the charts. Marketers from across the land hailed him as the sorcerer of storytelling.

The Epiphany of Anticipation

Max's journey through data-driven insights had led him to a profound revelation. Analytics wasn't just about numbers; it was about understanding the

dance of human behavior. By deciphering the patterns and embracing the quirks, he could anticipate
desires and mold his marketing spells accordingly.

And so, Marketer Max continued to enchant the
world with his insights, using data as his crystal ball
to foresee the whims of the marketing realm. As his
reputation as a storyteller and trendsetter grew, he
realized that the heart of analytics wasn't just in the
data; it was in the stories that the data whispered to
those who cared to listen.

And they all lived insightfully ever after.

Chapter 23: Creating Customer Personas for Tailored Engagement

O nce upon a time in the vibrant realm of marketing, where data danced and creativity reigned, Marketer Max found himself embarking on a new quest: the creation of customer personas for tailored engagement. With his trusty keyboard as his companion, Max delved deep into the world of personas, armed with his decades of experience and a sense of humor sharper than a well-crafted tagline.

As Max sipped his morning coffee, he pondered the essence of a persona. It was like throwing a grand party where each guest had their own quirks and preferences. Max chuckled to himself, imagining the persona party he was about to host in his mind.

The Extravagant Entertainer:

Max began by envisioning a lively character named Lucy, a party enthusiast with a penchant for throwing extravagant soirees. She represented the type of customer who loved the spotlight, craved the latest trends, and couldn't resist sharing her experiences on social media. Max could already see Lucy's Instagram feed filled with snapshots from her glamorous parties, each one a potential marketing opportunity. With Lucy in mind, Max knew that to engage her, he needed to present products and services as the "life of the party," capturing her attention with their uniqueness and trendiness.

The Practical Planner:

Next up, Max introduced Victor, a meticulous and organized individual who believed in planning every aspect of his life. Victor was the epitome of practicality, meticulously researching before making a purchase. Max imagined Victor meticulously comparing features, benefits, and reviews, as if crafting a detailed event itinerary. To win over Victor, Max realized he needed to provide clear, concise, and well-structured information that catered to Victor's analytical nature.

The Adventure Enthusiast:

Then came Olivia, a fearless adventurer with a passion for exploring the unknown. Max chuckled as he pictured Olivia skydiving one day and spelunking the next. Olivia represented the customers who sought unique experiences and were constantly seeking new challenges. Max knew that engaging Olivia meant appealing to her sense of discovery and presenting products and services as gateways to new and exciting experiences.

The Skeptical Detective:

As Max continued his persona party, he introduced Detective Alex, a skeptic by nature. Alex had a keen eye for detail and an ability to see through any marketing gimmicks. Max envisioned Alex researching products and services like a seasoned detective, cross-referencing information and seeking out unbiased reviews. To captivate Alex's interest, Max realized he needed to provide transparent and trustworthy information, backed by social proof and genuine customer testimonials.

The Social Connector:

Last but not least, Max welcomed Ethan, the social butterfly who effortlessly navigated between various social circles. Ethan thrived on building connections and valued products and services that facilitated social interactions. Max pictured Ethan as the life of every party, his energy infectious and his smile contagious. To engage Ethan, Max understood that he needed to emphasize the social aspects of products and services, highlighting how they could enhance connections and foster a sense of community.

With the persona party in full swing, Marketer Max marveled at the diverse characters he had conjured. Each persona represented a unique set of behaviors, preferences, and needs. As Max continued his journey through the world of tailored engagement, he carried the personas with him like cherished party guests, guiding his marketing strategies with insights and a touch of humor.

And so, dear reader, the tale of Marketer Max and his persona party teaches us that in the realm of market-ing, understanding and catering to the distinct per-sonalities of our customers can lead to engagement that's not just tailored, but unforgettable. Just like a well-thrown party, a well-crafted persona can light up the marketing landscape with laughter, insight, and a touch of magic.

24

Chapter 24: Feedback Loops: Continuous Improvement through Customer Input

In the mystical land of Marketingburg, where marketers roamed the digital realm armed with hashtags and taglines, there lived a wizardly marketer named Max. Max was known far and wide for his uncanny ability to concoct marketing spells that could turn even the most skeptical customers into loyal brand advocates. But there was one secret ingredient to his success that he held dearer than his trusty quill: Feedback Loops.

The tale of Max's adventures in Feedback Follies begins with a rather peculiar incident involving a grumpy troll and a mischievous parrot. Max had introduced a new product, the "Chameleon Chinos," which claimed to change color based on the wearer's mood. Marketing jargon aside, it was essentially a pair of really fancy pants. But the troll, who was always grumpy, gave them a resounding "meh."

Max, not one to be disheartened, embarked on a mission to decipher the troll's discontent. He initiated a Feedback Loop, which involved sending a charming survey to all his customers, seeking their opinions on the Chameleon Chinos. The survey was so engaging that even the parrot wanted in on the action. It dictated its thoughts to its owner, who then input the parrot's input into the survey. Max was truly surprised when he received a response that said, "Troll is right. Pants need more pizzazz!"

This unexpected feedback sparked an idea in Max's clever mind. He organized a "Pants Party" in the heart of Marketingburg. The event featured a runway show where models strutted their stuff in the Chameleon Chinos while carrying mood cards to demonstrate the color-changing effect. The troll, intrigued by the commotion, attended the party.

As the troll watched in awe, he noticed something peculiar: the pants did indeed change color, but only when exposed to a specific type of light. He immediately rushed to Max and exclaimed, "Pants only work under a disco ball light! Troll not wear disco ball to work!"

Max burst into laughter at the sight of the troll's frustration. He realized that he had missed a crucial detail during product development – the need for natural light to trigger the color change. Armed with this newfound insight, Max made some modifications to the Chameleon Chinos, ensuring they changed color even under regular lighting conditions. He rebranded them as "Mood Magic Chinos" and released them to resounding success.

The parrot, never one to miss out on a chance to offer its wisdom, squawked, "Parrot's picky opinion helped fix pants!"

And so, in this whimsical tale of Feedback Follies, Max learned that feedback loops weren't just about collecting data, but about uncovering unexpected insights and turning them into marketing magic. He continued to create enchanting campaigns that not only tickled his customers' fancy but also improved his products in ways he could never have imagined.

The moral of the story? In the realm of marketing, customer feedback isn't just valuable—it's a treasure trove of comedic mishaps and delightful surprises that can lead to unparalleled success. And as Max would often say, "A marketer without feedback is like a wizard without a wand – you might look impressive, but you're missing out on the real magic!"

VII

Empowering Customers to Articulate Their Needs

In the bustling marketplace of ideas, imagine a scenario where customers hold the brush to paint their desires. As a seasoned marketer and influencer, you understand the art of Empowering Customers to Articulate Their Needs. It's like orchestrating a symphony of wants, needs, and aspirations, giving them the spotlight they deserve. With the finesse of a maestro, you guide them through the maze of options, transforming vague wishes into eloquent demands.

Chapter 25: Educating Customers about Product/Service Features

I n the bustling world of marketing, where ideas are like fireflies, sometimes it's easy to get caught up in the dazzling dance of creativity. But wait, what's this? A chapter dedicated to the noble art of educating customers about product/service features? Well, dear readers, consider this chapter your map to navigate the intricate labyrinth of features and benefits.

Once upon a time in the realm of marketing, there lived a curious marketer named Max. Max had a knack for uncovering the hidden gems within products and services and presenting them in ways that made customers' eyes light up like a kid in a candy store. Max believed that every product had a story to tell, and it was his mission to bring those stories to life.

The Great Feature Reveal Extravaganza

One sunny morning, Max was tasked with promoting a cutting-edge gadget known as the "GizmoGlow." The GizmoGlow had more features than
a Swiss army knife and could do everything from
brewing coffee to predicting the weather. But there
was a problem: customers were overwhelmed by the
sheer number of features and didn't know where to
start.

Max, being the wise marketer that he was, decided
to throw a "Great Feature Reveal Extravaganza."
He rented out a glitzy event space and invited the
city's most influential people. The event began
with a dramatic curtain drop, revealing a massive
board filled with buttons, switches, and dials. Max,
dressed in a magician's robe, stepped forward and
declared, "Ladies and gentlemen, prepare to be
amazed!"

He started with a comical demonstration of the
GizmoGlow's "Instant Disco" feature. With a press
of a button, the gadget transformed the room into a
sparkling dance floor, complete with flashing lights
and groovy music. The audience erupted in laughter

and applause. Max had their attention.

Feature Storytelling Time

But Max knew that comedy was just the appetizer. For the main course, he dove into storytelling. Each feature became a character in a tale of its own. He narrated how the "WhisperQuiet" feature helped a busy mom finally get some rest while the kids played video games. He shared the heartwarming tale of a traveler who used the "Universal Translator" feature to connect with people from different corners of the world.

With every story, Max made sure to tie the features back to the customers' needs and desires. He didn't just talk about buttons and switches; he talked about solutions and experiences. The audience was hooked, and they couldn't wait to get their hands on the GizmoGlow.

The Lesson Learned

As Max wrapped up his presentation, he left the audience with a valuable lesson: Educating customers about product/service features wasn't about overwhelming them with technical details. It was about painting a picture of how those features could transform their lives. Max had taken a potentially dry topic and turned it into an unforgettable experience that left everyone entertained, informed, and ready to make a purchase.

So, dear readers, the next time you find yourself faced with the task of educating customers about product/service features, remember Max's tale. Put on your storytelling hat, sprinkle in a touch of magic, and watch as your customers become not just buyers, but believers in the power of what you're offering. And who knows, maybe you'll even get a standing ovation or two!

26

Chapter 26: Providing Resources for Informed Decision-Making

I n the bustling world of marketing, where decisions can feel as uncertain as a cat chasing a laser pointer, our intrepid marketer, Max, realized the importance of guiding clients towards informed decision-making. Armed with his decades of experience and a knack for turning even the most serious situation into a laughter-inducing escapade, Max embarked on a mission to create a chapter that would leave decision-making woes in the dust, with a side of chuckles.

Once upon a time, in a land of data-driven choices and analytics galore, Max found himself in a peculiar predicament. His client, a quirky startup named WhimsiTech, was grappling with the daunting task of choosing between two wildly different marketing strategies. On one hand, there was the tried-and-true guerrilla marketing approach, a whirlwind of creativity and surprise that could either result in a thunderous success or a bit of an awkward giggle. On the other hand, there was the calm waters of inbound lead generation, a methodical journey that felt as comfortable as a cozy sweater but lacked the flash of a sparkler.

Max, being the marketing maverick he was, decided to whip up a resource-rich strategy that would leave WhimsiTech equipped to make the most informed decision of their marketing lives. He knew he needed to channel his inner storytelling skills, so he gathered his team and started weaving a narrative that would make even the most indecisive marketer think twice before flipping a coin.

Picture this: Max assembled a team of metaphorical adventurers, each representing a different facet of the marketing world. There was Captain Curiosity, the explorer of uncharted territories who always sought new guerrilla tactics with the enthusiasm of a kid on a treasure hunt. Then there was Professor Precision, the data guru who could turn a spreadsheet into a symphony, orchestrating inbound strategies with meticulous attention to detail.

Max brought these characters to life through interactive workshops and engaging sessions. Captain Curiosity regaled the team with tales of guerrilla marketing exploits, like the time a flash mob of dancing penguins caused a sensation on social media, turning even the most stoic CEOs into toe-tapping fans. Meanwhile, Professor Precision regaled them with stories of how inbound strategies transformed skeptical website visitors into devoted subscribers, using data points like breadcrumbs leading to a digital feast.

As Max spun his stories, he sprinkled in hilarious anecdotes, like the time Captain Curiosity accidentally sent a box of whoopee cushions to a corporate office instead of the planned guerrilla mailer, resulting in unexpected laughter echoing through the halls of a Fortune 500 company. And who could forget the time Professor Precision mistook a campaign's decimal point for a comma, leading to an accidental million-dollar budget allocation to emojis in email subject lines?

Through laughter and enlightenment, Max's team at WhimsiTech began to see the merits of both approaches. They realized that guerrilla marketing could inject excitement into their brand and carve a niche in a crowded market, while inbound lead generation could provide a steady stream of qualified prospects. With the characters' stories as guidance, the team made an informed decision that combined the best of both worlds – a guerrilla-inspired inbound strategy, complete with surprise-laden emails and data-driven insights.

And so, Max's tale concludes with a valuable lesson: decision-making, in the realm of marketing and beyond, can be an adventure filled with twists, turns, and uproarious laughter. By providing resources that blend wisdom, whimsy, and data-driven insights, marketers like Max can equip their clients to make choices that lead to success stories worth sharing for years to come. So, remember, fellow marketers, embrace the journey, embrace the laughter, and most importantly, embrace the opportunity to guide others towards decisions that light up their paths like a firework display on a starry night.

27

Chapter 27: Encouraging Customer Feedback for Mutual Growth

I n the bustling realm of marketing, where campaigns swirled like caffeinated whirlwinds and strategies bloomed like digital daffodils, our wise Marketer Max found himself faced with a puzzle of peculiar proportions: how to encourage customer feedback for mutual growth. With a twinkle in his eye and a brainstorm swirling in his mind, Max embarked on a journey of wit and wisdom.

Once upon a time, in the land of Marketingville, Max stumbled upon a quaint little coffee shop known as "Beanstalk Brews." The aroma of freshly roasted beans beckoned passersby like a siren's song, and Max couldn't resist the temptation. He sauntered in, determined to blend in like a well-caffeinated chameleon.

As he sipped his mocha-choco-caramel-frappalatte, Max noticed a cleverly placed sign by the counter: "Tell Us Your Thoughts, Win a Year's Supply of Java Joy!" Curiosity piqued, Max observed a line of customers chatting animatedly with the barista, exchanging tales of their bean experiences. Max knew he had stumbled upon a goldmine of feedback brilliance.

After indulging in his caffeine conquest, Max decided to chat with the shop's owner, the jovial Joe. Over a cup of coffee (obviously), they hatched a plan that would make even the most seasoned marketers nod in approval.

Step 1: The Quirky Questionnaire Quest

Max remembered his niche influencer status on platforms like Quora, LinkedIn, and Instagram. Leveraging his charisma, he proposed the creation of quirky, gamified questionnaires that customers could answer in exchange for a virtual high-five or a meme-worthy GIF. Joe loved the idea, and they soon had questions like "If coffee were a superhero, what would its catchphrase be?" circulating online.

Step 2: The Feedback Fiesta

Turning the act of giving feedback into a carnival of delights, Max and Joe organized a "Feedback Fiesta" at Beanstalk Brews. Customers could spin a feedback wheel adorned with funny options like "I love your coffee more than my morning hair!" or "Your espresso shots are like a secret handshake with energy." The laughter was contagious, and so were the insights.

Step 3: The Appreciation Avalanche

Max knew that for mutual growth, appreciation was the key. So, he and Joe devised a way to showcase the feedback received. They transformed the wall near the counter into a "Wall of Witty Words," where customer comments were turned into playful artworks. This not only honored customers but also showcased the shop's dedication to improvement.

Step 4: The Bountiful Beans Exchange

Acknowledging that feedback was a two-way street, Max introduced the "Bountiful Beans Exchange." Customers who shared feedback were given "bean credits" that could be used for future purchases. This transformed feedback into a mutually beneficial cycle, where both the customers and the shop flourished.

As weeks turned into months, Beanstalk Brews became the talk of the town. The once-humble coffee shop now stood tall as a testament to the power of engaging, entertaining, and appreciating customers. Max's witty approach to encouraging feedback had not only brought growth to the shop but also woven a community of coffee enthusiasts who cherished each visit like a caffeinated adventure.

And so, dear reader, Max's tale reminds us that in the realm of marketing, a sprinkle of humor, a dash of gamification, and a generous helping of appreciation can turn even the most mundane task into a hilarious and insightful journey toward mutual growth. So go forth, fellow marketers, and dance the Feedback Fandango with your customers, for the best insights often wear the cloak of laughter.

Chapter 28: Customer Training: Enhancing User Knowledge and Confidence

O nce upon a time in the bustling world of marketing, a seasoned marketer named Max embarked on a journey to unlock the secrets of Customer Training. As he sipped his coffee and gazed out of his office window, Max knew that in this age of empowered customers, education was the key to success. Little did he know that his quest for customer training would lead him to create the "Aha!" Moment Academy.

Section 1: The Birth of the "Aha!" Moment Academy

Max's journey began when he received an email from a concerned client named Carla. Carla's company had a fantastic product, but their customers seemed to struggle with using it effectively. Max scratched his chin, realizing that customer knowledge and confidence were essential for long-term success. And thus, the "Aha!" Moment Academy was born.

Max started with a humorous analogy: "Teaching a customer is like teaching a fish to ride a bicycle – it's all about finding the right balance!" He shared the story of how, much like a fish discovering its balance on a bicycle, customers needed guidance to find their "Aha!" moments – those instances when they understood the true value of a product.

Section 2: The Quest for Customer Superheroes

In his next chapter, Max introduced the concept of "Customer Superheroes." He narrated the story of Emily, a regular office worker who transformed into a confident and knowledgeable user of a complex software through training. Max wove humor into the story, comparing Emily's journey to that of a mild-mannered reporter becoming Superman – complete with a cape and all!

Max's witty insights flowed as he explained that customer training was the secret sauce that turned ordinary users into champions of the product. He used examples of famous superheroes to illustrate how customer training elevated users from clueless novices to savvy champions, equipped to tackle any challenge that came their way.

Section 3: Crafting the Perfect Training Experience

As Max delved deeper into his chapter, he painted a vivid picture of crafting the perfect training experience. He drew parallels to a culinary adventure, comparing well-designed training to a gourmet meal – carefully planned, expertly prepared, and leaving customers craving for more.

Max's knack for storytelling shone through as he recounted his own experience attending a cooking class. He humorously described his attempts at creating a soufflé that looked more like a deflated balloon. By comparing his culinary mishap to the pitfalls of poorly designed training, Max emphasized the importance of clear communication, engaging content, and interactive learning to ensure a successful training journey.

Section 4: From "Aha!" Moments to ROI

In the final section of the chapter, Max connected

the dots between "Aha!" moments and Return on Investment (ROI). He recounted the tale of a business owner named Alex, who witnessed a dramatic increase in customer satisfaction and loyalty after implementing a comprehensive training program. With a twinkle in his eye, Max described how Alex's journey from skepticism to success mirrored the transformation of a caterpillar into a beautiful butterfly – a fitting analogy for the metamorphosis that effective training can bring about.

As Max concluded his chapter, he left readers with a hearty laugh and a newfound appreciation for the power of customer training. With his signature blend of humor, insight, and real-life examples, he had crafted a chapter that not only educated but entertained, much like a perfectly executed marketing campaign.

And so, the "Aha!" Moment Academy continued to flourish, churning out Customer Superheroes who conquered challenges and embraced their roles as product champions. Max's journey through the realm of Customer Training had not only enhanced user knowledge and confidence but had also left a trail of laughter and inspiration in its wake.

VIII

Navigating Challenging Customer Interactions

Navigating Challenging Customer Interactions is like orchestrating a quirky dance between business and emotions. Just as I've expertly navigated the realms of marketing, this guide draws from my two decades of experience to provide hilarious yet insightful strategies. Imagine a tightrope walk of wit and wisdom, where I, the maestro of marketing, teach you to tango with even the trickiest customers. Your stage? The digital sphere, where we transform disgruntled buyers into loyal fans.

Chapter 29: Dealing with Demanding and Difficult Customers

Once upon a time in the bustling city of Marketingville, there lived a seasoned marketer named Max. Max had seen it all – from skyrocketing campaigns to epic fails, but what really made him a legend among marketers was his uncanny ability to turn demanding and difficult customers into loyal brand advocates. It was a skill he had honed over his two decades in the field, and boy, did he have stories to tell!

Max sat back in his swivel chair, reminiscing about one particular encounter that became his shining example of how to tackle the most challenging customers. The sun was setting, casting a warm orange glow across his cluttered yet organized office. He adjusted his glasses and began to narrate:

"Picture this: a gloomy Monday morning, rain tapping on the windows like impatient fingers. My inbox pinged, and there it was – an email from a client, let's call him Mr. Grumpypants. His complaint was a mile long, filled with bold red fonts and enough exclamation marks to power a rocket. He was convinced that our latest campaign had ruined his life, and he demanded an immediate explanation.

Instead of panicking, I brewed a cup of strong coffee and picked up the phone. Taking a deep breath, I dialed Mr. Grumpypants' number. He answered with a growl that could have scared a lion. But I stayed cool, like a cucumber in a freezer.

'Hello, Mr. Grumpypants! It's Max from the marketing team. I got your email, and I'm truly sorry to hear about your concerns. I'd love to chat about it and figure out the best way to address your worries.'

Silence on the other end. And then, he exploded like a volcano. But instead of letting his anger consume me, I imagined he was a cartoon character with steam coming out of his ears. It might sound silly, but it helped me maintain my composure.

'Well, Max, this is absolutely unacceptable! Your

campaign has ruined my reputation, and I demand a refund!' he bellowed.

I leaned back in my chair, pretending to dodge his imaginary lava. 'Mr. Grumpypants, I understand your frustration, and I'm here to help. Can you walk me through the specific issues you've encountered?'

And there it was – the pivotal moment. Instead of arguing, I actively listened. I let him vent, all the while jotting down key points. By the time he finished, he was still annoyed, but the initial rage had subsided a bit.

I nodded, even though he couldn't see me. 'Thank you for sharing that. I truly appreciate your feedback. Let's work together to find a solution that not only addresses these concerns but also helps us improve our future campaigns.'

As we discussed the issues one by one, I offered insights and solutions. I even threw in a joke or two to lighten the mood. Slowly but surely, Mr. Grumpypants started to open up. It turned out that his main issue was a misunderstanding about the campaign's objectives. Once we clarified that, he was more receptive to the changes we could make.

By the end of the call, his tone had changed from furious to frustrated but hopeful. We ended with a plan – revisions to the campaign, a timeline for implementation, and a commitment to regular check-ins.

Over the next few weeks, I kept my promise. I sent him updates, shared progress reports, and included a few funny GIFs to keep things light. Gradually, Mr. Grumpypants transformed from a demanding client to a collaborative partner. He even recommended our services to a colleague, citing our responsiveness and dedication.

And that, my fellow marketers, is the power of turning a demanding and difficult customer into an advocate. It's not about taming a lion, but about understanding the roar and finding a way to dance to its beat."

Max leaned back, a satisfied smile on his face. The sun had dipped below the horizon, leaving behind a canvas of twinkling city lights. He hoped that his story would inspire marketers everywhere to approach even the most challenging customers with empathy, humor, and a dash of creativity.

And so, the legend of Max, the marketer who could

turn a grumpy bear into a loyal fan, continued to grow.

30

Chapter 30: Turning Customer Complaints into Opportunities

O nce upon a time in the bustling city of Marketingville, lived Marketer Max, a seasoned
expert with a bag full of tricks and a heart full
of determination. He had encountered his fair
share of challenges in the marketing realm, but
nothing could have prepared him for the incredible
transformation that customer complaints would
bring into his life.

Picture this: It was a cloudy Monday morning, and
Marketer Max was sipping his coffee while scrolling
through his emails. Among the cheerful messages
and new leads, there it was – a scathing email
from an unhappy customer. The subject line read:
"Your Product Ruined My Cat's Birthday Party!"
Max's eyes widened as he read through the lines

of disappointment and frustration. He couldn't help but chuckle at the sheer randomness of the complaint.

But Marketer Max was no ordinary marketer. He saw potential in every corner of the marketing universe. He leaned back in his chair, his creative wheels spinning faster than ever. "Turning Customer Complaints into Opportunities," he murmured to himself. This was a challenge he couldn't resist.

With a twinkle in his eye, Max drafted a response that combined humor, empathy, and an unexpected twist. He thanked the customer for their unique feedback and offered a heartfelt apology for the cat's ruined birthday party. He even attached a quirky cat meme, just to lighten the mood. Max knew that responding with authenticity could create a positive ripple.

But the story doesn't end here. A few days later, Max received a surprising response from the once-upset customer. It turned out that the customer was a blogger with a substantial following – a niche community of cat enthusiasts. The customer was so amused by Max's response that they decided to share the entire email interaction on their blog.

Marketer Max's creative approach had struck a chord with the customer and their readers. The blog post went viral in the cat-loving circles, bringing not only a wave of laughter but also a surge of interest in Max's brand. People admired the company's willingness to embrace humor and turn a negative experience into a positive one.

Max's inbox was flooded with messages from people who wanted to know more about his products, services, and his unique outlook on customer satisfaction. The unexpected turn of events had not only salvaged the situation but had turned it into a remarkable marketing opportunity.

From that day on, Marketer Max became known as the "Cat Whisperer" in the marketing world. He used this quirky title to his advantage, incorporating it into his branding and marketing materials. His response to the cat-related complaint became a legendary story that he shared during his speaking engagements and one-on-one consulting sessions. It was an embodiment of his philosophy – that every complaint, when handled creatively, could transform into a golden opportunity.

And so, dear readers, the tale of how Marketer Max turned a cat's birthday party fiasco into a marketing triumph serves as a testament to the power of embracing challenges with humor, empathy, and a dash of creativity. Remember, in the world of marketing, even a disgruntled cat can lead the way to unexpected success!

Chapter 31: Conflict Resolution: Finding Common Ground

Once upon a time in the bustling city of Marketingburg, there lived a clever marketer named Max. Max had navigated through the ever-changing landscape of marketing for decades, encountering a plethora of challenges and conflicts along the way. But there was one skill that set Max apart from the rest of the marketers: his knack for conflict resolution and finding common ground.

One sunny morning, Max received a call from a distressed client, Mr. Johnson, who was known for his passionate yet stubborn nature. Mr. Johnson's company was launching a new line of eco-friendly products, and he had a vision for an unconventional guerrilla marketing campaign involving skydiving squirrels. Yes, you heard that right—skydiving squirrels.

Max scratched his head in disbelief as he pondered how to address this seemingly absurd idea. He knew he needed to find a way to steer Mr. Johnson in a more effective direction. With a deep breath, Max arranged a meeting at a quirky café known for its extravagant milkshakes and avant-garde decor.

As Max sat across from Mr. Johnson, he carefully chose his words, "You know, Mr. Johnson, your idea of skydiving squirrels is truly... nuts! But let's think about this from a different angle. We both want to create buzz for your eco-friendly products, right?"

Mr. Johnson nodded enthusiastically, his eyes lighting up.

Max continued, "Instead of squirrels plummeting from the sky, how about we tap into the existing love people have for animals and nature? We could organize a 'Nature's Heroes' event where volunteers plant trees and clean up local parks. We'll tie it to your product launch, showcasing your commitment to the environment."

Mr. Johnson's furrowed brow slowly relaxed, and a smile crept onto his face. "That... that actually sounds like a great idea!"

As weeks went by, Max and Mr. Johnson collaborated closely on the Nature's Heroes event. They engaged influencers on Instagram, Quora, and LinkedIn to spread the word. The event turned out to be a massive success, with volunteers from all over the city participating. Local news outlets covered the heartwarming story of a company dedicated to making a positive impact on the environment.

During the event, Mr. Johnson approached Max with a grateful grin. "You were right, Max. I was a bit squirrel-brained with my initial idea. Thank you for guiding me toward something meaningful that aligned with our values."

Max chuckled, "Well, I've had my fair share of squirrelly ideas too. The key is to find common ground and align our visions with reality."

And so, Max's reputation as a master conflict resolver and visionary marketer grew even stronger. His ability to take seemingly outrageous ideas and transform them into impactful campaigns became the stuff of legends in Marketingburg. With every conflict that arose, Max knew that beneath the chaos, there was always a glimmer of common ground waiting to be discovered.

As the sun set on another successful campaign, Max leaned back in his chair, sipping his milkshake, and thought about how conflicts could be the stepping stones to innovation and collaboration, just like skydiving squirrels turned into environmental champions.

32

Chapter 32: Cultivating Patience and Resilience in Customer Interactions

I n the realm of marketing, where the digital dragons breathe fire and the algorithms play tricks, Marketer Max embarked on a treacherous journey to cultivate the virtues of patience and resilience in the land of customer interactions. Armed with his trusty quill and the battle-tested shield of experience, Max ventured forth to conquer the trials that awaited him.

The Temptation of Swift Replies

In the bustling town of Inboxville, where messages flowed like a river in flood, Max encountered the alluring enchantress known as Instant Gratification. She whispered sweet promises of rapid responses and immediate resolutions, tempting him to forsake the virtues he sought. Max knew that hasty replies often led to misunderstanding, like the time a well-meaning mage cast a spell of autocorrect, turning "special discount" into "spectral disco." The lesson was clear: swift replies might appease the moment, but patience forged true understanding.

The Mirage of Quick Conversions

On a dusty path through the Desert of Impatience, Max stumbled upon the Mirage of Quick Conversions. This deceptive illusion danced with seductive numbers, promising a mirage of instant success. Tempted by the mirage, Max once launched a campaign that promised "overnight stardom" to his customers. However, the only stardom he achieved was a constellation of unsatisfied customers who felt deceived. It was then that Max realized that genuine connections took time to nurture, like tending to a magical garden. Patience in cultivating relationships yielded the sweetest fruits.

The Battle of the Unsubscribes

In the realm of Social Media Peaks, Max encountered the Mischievous Goblin of Negative Comments. This cunning creature thrived on inciting emotional responses, but Max saw through its tricks. Once, the goblin provoked him into a heated debate, and Max's words became more fiery than a dragon's breath. The battle escalated until the realm's wise sages reminded Max of the ancient saying: "An angry reply to a goblin's jest is like casting fire on a straw roof." Max learned that resilience meant choosing battles wisely and turning negativity into opportunities for growth.

The Fortress of Feedback

At the heart of the Feedback Mountains, Max found the enigmatic Fortress of Constructive Criticism. Its walls were adorned with posters that bore witness to his mistakes and failures. As Max entered the fortress, he realized that criticism was a map to self-improvement, much like a treasure map leading to a dragon's hoard. Instead of taking it personally, Max listened and learned, much like the time he had misunderstood a market trend and ended up promoting "medieval fashion" in a futuristic world. Embracing feedback became his secret potion of resilience.

The Resilience Elixir

After navigating the trials and tribulations, Marketer Max discovered the Resilience Elixir hidden in the Cave of Reflection. This potent potion was brewed from equal parts of experience and self-awareness, stirred with a dash of humor. Max's journey had taught him that setbacks were not signs of defeat, but stepping stones to success. He knew that every failed campaign was a chapter in the Book of Learning, and every challenge was a chance to rewrite the story with humor and resilience.

And so, with patience as his guiding star and resilience as his shield, Marketer Max continued his noble quest in the ever-changing world of marketing. His encounters with Instant Gratification, the Mirage of Quick Conversions, the Mischievous Goblin of Negative Comments, the Fortress of Constructive Criticism, and the Resilience Elixir shaped him into a legendary figure whose tales inspired marketers and adventurers for generations to come.

IX

Building Lasting Customer Relationships

33

Chapter 33: The Value of Customer Trust and Loyalty

O nce upon a time, in the bustling city of Marketingville, lived a wise old marketer named Max. Max was not your average marketer – he had a magical touch when it came to building relationships with customers. He believed that the heart of any successful marketing strategy was rooted in the solid foundation of customer trust and loyalty. And so, Chapter 33 of his marketing journey unfolded, exploring "The Value of Customer Trust and Loyalty."

In the land of Marketingville, there was a famous marketplace known as "Trustworthiness Square." This square was where businesses and customers converged, each transaction a potential stepping stone towards building trust. Max would often visit this square to witness the magic of trust and loyalty in action.

One sunny morning, Max strolled into Trustworthiness Square with a curious gleam in his eye. He observed a vendor named Vivian who sold the most delightful handcrafted toys. Vivian was known far and wide for her exceptional quality and honest dealings. She would often share stories about her customers' children and their joy upon receiving her toys.

Max approached Vivian and struck up a conversation. "Vivian, your customers truly adore you. What's your secret?"

Vivian smiled and replied, "It's all about trust, Max. When customers know that you have their best interests at heart, they become more than just customers – they become loyal friends. I've seen parents bring their children to my stall, and I can see the trust in their eyes. They know that my toys are safe and made with care."

Max nodded, intrigued. He then spotted a group of young entrepreneurs nearby who were just starting their businesses. They were discussing strategies to increase sales quickly.

With a mischievous grin, Max decided to play a little game. He approached the group and said, "Hey, have you heard of the 'Trust Domino Effect'?"

The young entrepreneurs looked puzzled and asked, "What's that?"

Max leaned in, his eyes twinkling, and began his tale. "Imagine trust as a domino. When you build it, it becomes the first piece that sets off a chain reaction. Once customers trust you, they're more likely to recommend your business to others. These recommendations create a ripple effect, drawing in even more customers who trust you from the start."

As Max shared his story, the young entrepreneurs were captivated. They realized that trust was like a treasure chest – the more they invested in it, the greater the rewards. They started rethinking their approach, focusing on building relationships rather than just making sales.

Back at Max's own marketing dojo, he continued to spread the wisdom of trust and loyalty. He shared stories of businesses that went the extra mile to ensure customer satisfaction. There was the tale of a small bakery that remembered every customer's birthday and would surprise them with a special cake. And then there was the tech company that offered exceptional after-sales support, turning customers into brand advocates.

In the end, Max's journey through Chapter 33 emphasized that building customer trust and loyalty was more than just a strategy – it was a way of life for successful marketers. Like the pieces of a puzzle, every interaction, every promise kept, and every genuine effort contributed to the masterpiece of trust. And as Max looked out into the horizon, he knew that his adventures in Trustworthiness Square were far from over, for the bonds of customer trust and loyalty were unbreakable, just like the magic of storytelling in marketing.

And so, dear reader, remember the lessons Max learned in Chapter 33: Build trust like you're crafting a masterpiece, and nurture loyalty like you're tending to a precious garden. For in the world of marketing, the value of customer trust and loyalty is a treasure beyond measure.

Chapter 34: Going Beyond Transactions: Creating Emotional Connections

O nce upon a time, in the bustling city of Marketingville, lived Marketer Max, a seasoned
marketing guru with more tricks up his sleeve than
a magician at a circus. With his trusty quill pen
in one hand and a cup of coffee in the other, Max
embarked on a journey to explore the mystical land
of emotional connections in the realm of marketing.

It was a sunny morning when Max found himself
in the heart of the city, surrounded by billboards,
flashing lights, and bustling crowds. He decided to
pay a visit to the "Emotion Emporium," a store that
sold an array of emotions ranging from delight to
nostalgia, all bottled up and ready to be infused into

marketing campaigns.

As Max stepped into the store, a quirky shopkeeper named Emilia greeted him with a mischievous grin. "Welcome to the Emotion Emporium, dear Max! What brings you to our humble abode?"

Max chuckled, "Well, Emilia, I've heard that emotions are the secret sauce of successful marketing. I'm here to uncover the magic behind creating emotional connections with customers."

Emilia nodded knowingly, guiding Max through shelves filled with emotional vials. "You see, Max, marketing isn't just about selling products or services. It's about forging a bond, a connection, with your audience. Imagine you're throwing a grand masquerade ball, and your customers are the guests. How do you want them to feel?"

Max's eyes gleamed with understanding. "Ah, I get it! Just like a memorable party, a successful marketing campaign should evoke emotions that resonate with the customers' desires and dreams."

Emilia clapped her hands in delight. "Exactly! Let me share a tale with you, Max. Once, there was a shoe company that didn't just sell footwear; they sold dreams of conquering new horizons. Their commercials depicted people embarking on epic adventures, all while wearing their shoes. They didn't just sell shoes; they sold the thrill of exploration."

Max snapped his fingers, "That's brilliant! They transformed a simple product into a vessel of aspiration and emotion."

Emilia winked, "Now, let's add a dash of nostalgia to the mix. Imagine a candy company that revived the flavors of childhood in their advertisements. With each candy, they sold a trip down memory lane, allowing customers to relive the joy of their younger days."

Max grinned, "Nostalgia is a powerful tool, isn't it? It taps into emotions that are deeply ingrained in our hearts."

Emilia twirled a vial of joy in her fingers. "Indeed! And let's not forget humor. A fast-food chain used clever humor to become a part of people's lives. They didn't just sell burgers; they sold belly laughs and shared moments."

Max chuckled, "Humor is a universal language that breaks down barriers and creates connections."

163

Emilia handed Max a vial of inspiration. "And finally, inspiration. A tech company didn't just market gadgets; they marketed a future where individuals could achieve their wildest dreams using their products."

Max nodded, "Inspiration motivates action. It propels customers towards a better version of themselves."

As Max left the Emotion Emporium, he couldn't help but feel inspired himself. Armed with a new perspective, he set out to infuse his marketing strategies with emotions that would not just attract customers, but also create lasting connections.

And so, dear readers, the tale of Marketer Max teaches us that beyond transactions lie the treasures of emotional connections. Just as a symphony requires different notes to create a masterpiece, successful marketing campaigns require a symphony of emotions to resonate with the hearts and minds of customers. So, the next time you craft a campaign, remember the lessons learned from Max's journey and let emotions be your guiding light.

And thus, the quill of wisdom penned another chapter in Marketer Max's adventurous journey, leaving

a trail of laughter, insight, and emotionally charged
marketing campaigns in its wake.

Chapter 35: Customer Retention Strategies for Long-Term Success

I n the realm of marketing, where the winds of change blow like viral memes on social media, every seasoned marketer knows that acquiring new customers is just the beginning of the journey. Ah, Customer Retention, the mythical beast that many have tried to tame, but only a few have truly conquered. So, gather 'round fellow marketers, for I shall regale you with tales of Customer Retention Strategies for Long-Term Success.

Once upon a time, in a digital kingdom not so far away, there lived a wise marketer named Max. Max had battled countless marketing challenges and had slain dragons of data analysis and goblins of ad targeting. But the most fearsome challenge of all was retaining those hard-won customers, ensuring they didn't vanish into the fog of indifference.

Tale of the Loyal Quests: Max knew that customers aren't just numbers on a spreadsheet; they're adventurers seeking value. Max embarked on a journey to create loyalty programs that would rival the quests of old. Just like knights earning their spurs, customers earned rewards for their loyalty. Max's company, "Valor Mart," offered loyalty points for every purchase. The more points customers amassed, the more epic the rewards became. And so, customers returned to Valor Mart's kingdom, not for the mere transaction, but for the thrill of the adventure and the treasure that awaited them.

Sorcery of Personalization: Max also dabbled in the arcane arts of personalization. He knew that customers crave a magical experience that makes them feel unique. With the help of enchanted algorithms, Max's marketing campaigns addressed customers by name and recommended products based on their past choices. Customers marveled at the mystical accuracy and felt as if Max's company could read their minds. "By the powers of Big Data and a sprinkle of fairy dust," Max would chuckle.

The Chronicles of Communication: But Customer

Retention wasn't all about magic and quests. It was also about consistent communication. Max penned a series of engaging emails that wasn't just sales pitches but delightful anecdotes. These emails would drop into customers' inboxes like messages from a trusted bard, sharing stories of Valor Mart's latest conquests and offerings. Customers eagerly awaited each chapter of this ongoing saga, feeling like they were part of a grand narrative.

The Fabled Feedback Loop: Max knew that even in the most magical of kingdoms, things could go awry. So, he established a fabled feedback loop. Whenever a customer ventured forth to cancel their subscription, Max's team would reach out with curiosity, not desperation. They sought to understand the reasons behind the departure, aiming to mend their mistakes and earn back their loyalty. Customers were stunned by the genuine concern and often chose to stay, feeling valued and heard.

And thus, Max's tales of Customer Retention Strategies for Long-Term Success spread far and wide, inspiring marketers across the land. Through loyalty quests, personalized enchantments, engaging chronicles, and the power of the feedback loop, Max had managed to retain customers like never before. His marketing prowess was celebrated in ballads and whispered in marketing guilds, becoming a legendary example of how to keep customers coming back for more.

Dear fellow marketer, take heed of Max's tales, for in this ever-evolving landscape, the quest for Customer Retention is a noble one. Arm yourself with creativity, data-driven insights, and the desire to craft experiences that customers will cherish. And remember, like Max, you too can forge bonds that withstand the test of time, turning one-time buyers into lifelong companions on your marketing journey.

36

Chapter 36: Surprise and Delight: Exceeding Customer Expectations

O nce upon a time, in the bustling world of marketing, there lived a seasoned marketer named Max. Max was renowned for his 20 years of experience, his impressive collection of 103 books on Amazon, and his captivating presence as an orator and niche influencer on various platforms like Quora, LinkedIn, and even Instagram. He had the power to make marketing strategies come alive with a touch of his unique flair.

One sunny morning, Max found himself facing a new challenge: how to create a chapter on "Surprise and Delight: Exceeding Customer Expectations." Armed with his expertise in gamification, guerrilla marketing, and lead generation, Max decided to weave a story that would make even the most stoic marketer chuckle and ponder.

In the city of Brandington, a small coffee shop named "Perk Haven" stood as a testament to the magic of surprise and delight. The owner, Lily, was a marketing enthusiast herself and had attended one of Max's workshops on gamification. With Max's teachings in mind, she hatched a plan to turn her coffee shop into a hub of unexpected joy.

Lily realized that in the era of online reviews and social media buzz, making customers feel special was the key to winning their hearts. So, armed with her creativity and a dash of quirkiness, Lily began her mission. Every week, she introduced a "Mystery Mug Day," where customers who ordered a certain drink were given a mug with a surprise message or a quirky doodle. The social media frenzy that followed was astonishing.

One day, a customer named Alex walked into Perk Haven. He ordered his usual cappuccino and received a mug with a doodle of a caffeine molecule riding a skateboard. Alex burst into laughter and posted a picture of the mug on Instagram. The post went viral, and suddenly, people from neighboring cities were flocking to Perk Haven to experience the delight themselves.

Max, always curious about innovative marketing strategies, happened to be in Brandington for a speaking engagement. Intrigued by the buzz surrounding Perk Haven, he decided to pay a visit. As he sipped on his cappuccino, he noticed a group of customers engaged in a coffee bean guessing game. Lily had hidden a jar filled with coffee beans, and the person who guessed the closest number won a free coffee for a month.

Impressed by the gamification element and the sheer joy on customers' faces, Max struck up a conversation with Lily. He learned that she had used her HubSpot inbound lead generation certification to gather email addresses from these games, and she would send personalized surprise offers to her customers, keeping them engaged and excited.

Max couldn't resist sharing this story during his next speaking engagement. He painted a vivid picture of Perk Haven, where every customer was not just a transaction but a participant in a delightful experience. The audience roared with laughter and applause, and soon, Max's talk became the talk of the marketing community.

And so, dear readers, the tale of Surprise and Delight doesn't end here. It continues to inspire marketers like Max and entrepreneurs like Lily to push the boundaries of customer engagement. Just like Max, who sprinkled humor and insight into his storytelling, remember to add your unique touch to surprise and delight your customers, making their journey with your brand a memorable adventure.

X

Future Trends in Customer Engagement

In a world where hashtags trend faster than coffee runs, customer engagement is the magical wand every marketer covets. Picture this: as a seasoned marketer with more books than your bookshelf can handle, you're no stranger to the dance of engagement. Now, let's tango into the future!

Customers are no longer frogs waiting for a prince; they're queens and kings demanding experiences that whisk them off their feet.

37

Chapter 37: AI and Personalization: The Future of Customer Understanding

O nce upon a time, in the bustling world of marketing, Marketer Max found himself at a crossroads. He had witnessed the evolution of marketing strategies over the years, from traditional billboards to social media blitzes. But now, a new star was rising in the marketing sky: Artificial Intelligence, or AI, was taking center stage.

Max's curiosity was piqued, and he dove headfirst into exploring the realm of AI-powered personalization. He realized that AI had the potential to transform customer understanding like never before. As he sipped his coffee, he recalled a story that perfectly illustrated this shift.

In the heart of a quaint little town, there was a bakery named "Sweet Serendipity." The owner, Betty, was a warm and friendly lady who had been running the bakery for years. She knew most of her regular customers by name and always greeted them with a smile. But there was one thing she struggled with: remembering everyone's favorite pastries.

Enter AI-powered personalization. Betty decided to implement an AI system that analyzed customer preferences, buying patterns, and even social media activity. Armed with this data, the AI suggested personalized pastry recommendations for each customer. The results were nothing short of magical.

One day, a customer named Alex walked into the bakery. The AI recognized Alex as a chocolate enthusiast with a penchant for trying new flavors. It recommended a delectable triple-layered chocolate cake infused with exotic spices. As Alex took the first bite, a look of sheer delight spread across their face. Betty watched in awe as the AI not only delighted a customer but also boosted sales.

Marketer Max mused, "AI not only understands our customers better than ever, but it also empowers us to deliver personalized experiences that leave a lasting impact." He envisioned himself as Betty, applying AI-driven insights to his marketing strategies, and he couldn't help but chuckle at the thought of his digital assistant crafting witty ads tailored to individual preferences.

But Max knew that AI wasn't just about pastry recommendations and catchy ad copy. It was about understanding customers on a deeper level. He remembered another story he had heard about a shoe company that used AI to revolutionize its customer interactions.

The shoe company, "SoleMate," had struggled with sizing issues for years. Customers would often receive shoes that didn't quite fit, leading to frustrating returns and exchanges. With the power of AI, SoleMate introduced a virtual fitting room. Customers could scan their feet using a smartphone app, and the AI would accurately recommend the perfect shoe size.

Max grinned at the thought of AI-powered shoe fittings saving the day. He envisioned a hilarious scenario where an AI shoe butler escorted customers through a digital fitting room, complete with holographic shoes that danced in front of them. It was as if AI had breathed life into customer service.

As Max penned the chapter content, he couldn't help but marvel at the endless possibilities AI brought to the table. From personalized email campaigns that made customers chuckle to chatbots that answered queries with a dash of humor, AI was shaping a future where marketing was not just about selling products but about creating delightful experiences.

And so, with a mix of humor, insight, and real-life anecdotes, Marketer Max painted a vivid picture of how AI and personalization were transforming the landscape of customer understanding. As he closed his laptop, he couldn't help but feel excited about the journey ahead, where AI and marketing danced together in a harmonious symphony of innovation and connection.

38

Chapter 38: Augmented Reality in Customer Decision-Making

Once upon a time in the bustling city of Markethaven, where marketers roamed the digital plains in search of elusive customers, a peculiar trend emerged that would forever alter the way decisions were made. Augmented Reality (AR), the enchanting sorceress of the marketing realm, stepped onto the stage, and oh, what a spectacle it was!

Meet Jack, a savvy shopper who prided himself on his ability to spot a great deal from miles away. He had heard whispers of this newfangled thing called Augmented Reality, but he was a skeptic. Little did he know, his journey through the realm of decision-making was about to take a hilarious twist.

One fine day, while sipping his coffee at Café Imagi-natte, Jack noticed a curious poster on the wall. It promised an AR-powered shopping experience like no other. Chuckling to himself, he decided to give it a shot, thinking it would be an amusing diversion from his routine. He donned the AR glasses provided and suddenly found himself in a whimsical world of virtual aisles and pixelated products.

As Jack navigated the fantastical marketplace, he stumbled upon a virtual stand offering a variety of hats. "Why not?" he thought, and tried on a digital fedora. To his surprise, the hat perched perfectly on his head, casting a virtual shadow over his virtual eyebrows. With a chuckle, he snapped a selfie and sent it to his friends, who responded with a chorus of emojis.

But the real hilarity unfolded when Jack wandered into the "Try Before You Buy" AR zone. As he approached a holographic car, he couldn't resist sitting behind the virtual wheel. Ignoring the con-fused glances of café patrons, he revved the invisible engine and zoomed through the streets of the digital city, all while sipping his coffee. Passersby couldn't help but burst into laughter at the sight of Jack's enthusiastic steering of thin air.

Meanwhile, across the café, Lily, a fellow shopper, had been observing Jack's antics with an amused smile. She had experienced AR shopping before and had already found the perfect pair of shoes for herself. But seeing Jack's infectious enthusiasm, she decided to approach him. "You seem to be having quite the adventure," she said, stifling a laugh.

Jack, removing his AR glasses and grinning, replied, "Oh, you have no idea! I've just test-driven a virtual car and worn an imaginary hat that looked suspiciously real!" They both shared a hearty laugh.

As they chatted, Lily shared her own AR shopping escapades, recounting how she had virtually placed furniture in her apartment before making a purchase. Jack was intrigued. He realized that beyond the hilarity, there was a layer of real value in AR-based decision-making. The ability to visualize products in context and interact with them virtually was like a whimsical guide on his shopping journey.

From that day on, Jack became a staunch advocate of Augmented Reality in the realm of customer decision-making. He even wrote a comically insightful post on his favorite platform, Quora, recounting his AR misadventures and the unexpected connections he had made through the laughter-inducing experiences.

And so, in the city of Markethaven, Augmented Reality transformed from a marketing trend to a delightful adventure that bridged the gap between the real and the virtual. The dance of AR in customer decision-making continued to unfold, infusing the world of marketing with a touch of whimsy, a dash of hilarity, and a heap of insightful value. And Jack? Well, he became known as the "AR Adventurer," inspiring shoppers far and wide to embark on their own virtual escapades.

So, dear reader, the next time you put on those AR glasses, remember Jack's story and embrace the laughter, insight, and real-life connections that Augmented Reality can bring to your decision-making journey. After all, in the realm of marketing, a little bit of magic can go a long way!

39

Chapter 39: Sustainability and Ethical Considerations in Customer Choices

O nce upon a time, in the bustling realm of marketing, where clever slogans and flashy ads reigned supreme, a new chapter emerged - Chapter 39: Sustainability and Ethical Considerations in Customer Choices. Our protagonist, Marketer Max, found himself standing at the crossroads of commerce and conscience, ready to embark on a journey that would change the course of his marketing adventures.

In a world driven by consumerism, Marketer Max had witnessed the rise and fall of fads, the ebb and flow of trends, but now a new wave was crashing onto the shores of marketing - the wave of sustainability and ethical awareness. As he gazed upon the horizon, he realized that customers were no longer just buying products; they were buying stories, values, and a connection to a higher purpose.

Max had always believed in the power of storytelling, and this new chapter was a golden opportunity. He rolled up his sleeves and set out to create campaigns that didn't just tout product features, but also the eco-friendly practices and ethical sourcing behind them. He recalled the time he saw a fellow marketer trying to sell a "100% organic" widget that was wrapped in layers of non-recyclable plastic. Max chuckled as he envisioned a cartoon version of himself shaking his head in disbelief.

With a dash of humor and a sprinkle of insight, Marketer Max crafted a campaign that showcased the journey of a product from its humble origins to the hands of a customer. He used colorful visuals to depict the journey, from the sustainable farms where raw materials were sourced to the fair-trade factories where they were transformed. And let's not forget the whimsical animation of a plastic bottle shedding tears as it learned about the joys of recycling.

Max's campaign resonated with customers on a deeper level. They weren't just buying a product; they were investing in a greener, more ethical future.

And as the sales numbers soared, Max couldn't help but chuckle at the irony of a profit-driven approach actually making the world a better place.

But the journey wasn't without its challenges. Max faced skeptics who accused him of jumping on the bandwagon of "greenwashing." He remembered one fiery debate with a fellow marketer who scoffed at his efforts, claiming that consumers would see through the facade. Max, with a twinkle in his eye, responded with a tale of his own. He recounted the fable of the boy who cried wolf, highlighting the importance of genuine intentions and the long-term commitment to sustainability.

As Max continued to navigate the uncharted waters of sustainable marketing, he discovered an unexpected ally - the influencer community he had built over the years. Leveraging his connections on Quora, LinkedIn, and Instagram, he brought together a group of passionate environmentalists and ethical enthusiasts. Together, they became the Green Gurus and Ethical Explorers, a formidable force that not only spread awareness but also inspired others to make mindful choices.

And so, dear reader, as we close the pages of Chapter 39, we leave behind a world that's a bit more conscious, a tad more responsible, and definitely more entertaining. Marketer Max's journey showed us that marketing isn't just about selling products; it's about selling stories, values, and the promise of a brighter tomorrow. So, the next time you see a product boasting about its sustainability, remember the tale of Marketer Max and the Green Gurus, and know that behind every claim lies a marketer's quest to make a difference, one witty campaign at a time.

40

Chapter 40: Adapting to Changing Customer Behavior in Dynamic Markets

O nce upon a time, in the ever-evolving realm of marketing, lived our protagonist, Marketer Max. With over two decades of experience tucked under his marketing belt, Max knew that the only constant in the world of marketing was change itself. It was a sunny morning as Max sat down to write the next chapter of his marketing saga – Chapter 40: Adapting to Changing Customer Behavior in Dynamic Markets.

In this chapter, Max decided to share his insights with a dose of humor, a sprinkle of wisdom, and a pinch of his own experiences. He chuckled as he reminisced about the time he introduced a new product to the market, only to find out that customers were more interested in its quirky packaging than its actual features. Lesson learned: sometimes, it's not just about what's inside the box, but also about how you present it.

Max remembered another instance where he was consulting for a company specializing in retro-inspired fashion. Just when they thought they had cracked the code to appeal to their target audience, the tide shifted. Suddenly, futuristic designs were all the rage, leaving Max's client scratching their heads. Max's advice? "Don't just follow trends; be ready to set them."

Drawing inspiration from his own journey, Max crafted a story within the chapter. He introduced a fictional character named Lucy, who was a marketing whiz but found herself puzzled by the ever-changing behavior of her customers. Lucy's business, "Lucy's Luscious Cookies," was facing a slump despite its delicious treats.

With his signature humor, Max described Lucy's attempts to understand her customers' shifting preferences. From conducting surveys to attending focus groups, Lucy's efforts seemed to resemble a comedy show more than a marketing campaign.

But Max's point was clear: adapting to customer behavior required both creativity and persistence.

Max also shared a real-life anecdote from his niche influencer days on Quora. A user once asked about the effectiveness of traditional marketing in the age of social media dominance. Max responded with a witty tale of two marketers – Traditional Tom and Social Sam. Tom insisted on sticking to billboards, while Sam embraced Instagram influencers. The twist? Sam's sales skyrocketed, while Tom's billboards were mistaken for ancient hieroglyphics by the youth. Max's advice was loud and clear: "Embrace change, or risk becoming a marketing relic!"

As the chapter unfolded, Max delved into the art of harnessing data and technology. He recounted how he used gamification to engage his audience, turning mundane surveys into exciting challenges. Max also provided insights into guerrilla marketing tactics, such as the time he organized a flash mob to promote a new product launch. Passersby were so captivated by the spectacle that they forgot they were watching a marketing stunt!

Throughout the chapter, Max seamlessly blended humor, real-life anecdotes, and insightful lessons.

He urged marketers to stay curious, embrace change, and remember that even in the most dynamic markets, authenticity and creativity were the secret ingredients to success. With a final witty twist, Max signed off the chapter, leaving readers both amused and enlightened.

And so, the tale of Marketer Max continued, as he ventured into the ever-shifting landscape of marketing, armed with his decades of experience, a quirky sense of humor, and an unwavering passion for adapting to the changing behavior of customers in dynamic markets.

About the Author

Once upon a time in the realm of marketing mastery, there lived a luminary named Krishna Mohan Avancha. With a quiver full of marketing arrows and a mind as sharp as a perfectly crafted tagline, Krishna had penned 104 books that danced off the pages and into the hearts of readers. Among his literary treasures stood a masterpiece titled "Changing Customer Landscapes!" – a book so insightful that even the most enigmatic algorithms would give it a double thumbs-up.

Having roamed the marketing battlefield for over two decades, Krishna was not just a marketer; he was a legend whispered about around campfires of marketing seminars. He was the sage who could gamify a situation, turning it from a mundane task to an engaging adventure. Guerrilla marketing was his secret art – he could make a billboard disappear and reappear in your dreams, leaving you wondering if you were awake or in the middle of a captivating campaign.

Lead generation was Krishna's playfield, where he danced through digital landscapes like a lead-magnet maestro. He was so inbound-certified that even the internet's algorithms took notes from him. HubSpot itself bestowed upon him the coveted title of "Inbound Lead Generation Guru."

But wait, there's more! Krishna had a flair for SEO that made search engines blush. He knew how to make Google's algorithms fall head over heels for his content, as if they were in a romantic comedy where keywords were the love notes exchanged.

And customer satisfaction? Ah, Krishna was the fairy godmother of delighted customers. He knew that keeping customers happy was like tending to a delicate garden. He watered it with attention, pruned away negativity, and watched it bloom with loyalty.

But Krishna's influence didn't end with ink and paper. He was a digital Pied Piper, leading his followers through the social media maze. Quora, Instagram, and every platform that held a megaphone saw him standing tall as an influencer, sharing wisdom with a sprinkle of wit.

When the stars aligned and time allowed, Krishna transformed into a podcaster and YouTuber. His voice resonated through earbuds, and his videos turned viewers into his marketing disciples.

So, the next time you're lost in the labyrinth of marketing mayhem, remember the name Krishna Mohan Avancha. He's the marketer who could gamify your troubles, guerrilla your doubts, generate leads like a digital sorcerer, and turn SEO into poetry. And as for customer satisfaction? Well, let's just say that Krishna could make even the grumpiest customer break into a satisfied dance.

You can connect with me on:
- ◉ http://recruitdo.rf.gd
- 𝕏 https://twitter.com/avanchak
- ⓕ https://www.facebook.com/avanchakm
- ✇ https://www.linkedin.com/in/avanchak